# NONGOVERNMENTAL ORGANIZATION (NGO) PROFESSIONALS

## PRACTICAL CAREER GUIDES

**Series Editor:** Kezia Endsley

# NONGOVERNMENTAL ORGANIZATION (NGO) PROFESSIONALS

*A Practical Career Guide*

## TRACY BROWN HAMILTON

ROWMAN & LITTLEFIELD
*Lanham • Boulder • New York • London*

Published by Rowman & Littlefield
An imprint of The Rowman & Littlefield Publishing Group, Inc.
4501 Forbes Boulevard, Suite 200, Lanham, Maryland 20706
www.rowman.com

6 Tinworth Street, London, SE11 5AL, United Kingdom

British Library Cataloguing in Publication Information Available

**Library of Congress Cataloging-in-Publication Data**

Names: Hamilton, Tracy Brown, author.
Title: Nongovernmental organization (NGO) professionals : a practical career guide / Tracy Brown Hamilton.
Description: Lanham : Rowman & Littlefield, 2021. | Series: Practical career guides | Includes bibliographical references. | Summary: "This book walks you through the steps of deciding whether an NGO career is right for you and understanding the types of roles available within the sector."—Provided by publisher.
Identifiers: LCCN 2020034576 (print) | LCCN 2020034577 (ebook) | ISBN 9781538144732 (paperback) | ISBN 9781538144749 (epub)
Subjects: LCSH: Vocational guidance. | Non-governmental organizations. | Professions.
Classification: LCC HF5381 .H131956 2021 (print) | LCC HF5381 (ebook) | DDC 361.7/7023—dc23
LC record available at https://lccn.loc.gov/2020034576
LC ebook record available at https://lccn.loc.gov/2020034577

♾️™ The paper used in this publication meets the minimum requirements of American National Standard for Information Sciences—Permanence of Paper for Printed Library Materials, ANSI/NISO Z39.48-1992.

# Contents

# Introduction

## So You Want a Career in the NGO Sector

*W*elcome to the world of nongovernmental organizations, or NGOs! This book is the ideal starting point for understanding the various careers available to you within the NGO sector, finding out which direction is the best fit for you, and discovering what path you should follow to ensure you have all the training, education, and experience needed to succeed in your future career goals.

The NGO sector is a broad one, with different NGOs tackling various issues nationally and around the world. The types of roles and careers available within an NGO are equally diverse. Although NGOs do not share the same goals or means of measuring success as corporate for-profit organizations, they do operate with many of the same roles, such as marketing, legal departments, product development, field research, and finance. Having so many paths to choose from is exciting, but it can also make it difficult to choose which is the best fit for you.

## A Career in the NGO Sector

Because NGOs rely on so many areas of expertise to function successfully, almost any career path could be one that could be pursued in an NGO setting. Covering them all is therefore beyond the scope of this book. It will, however, address the most common careers and those most specific to the missions of NGOs. The careers covered in this book include:

- Management and operations
- Policy development

- Research
- Personnel and human resources
- Campaigning and fundraising
- Communications and public relations
- Volunteer management
- Grant writing

Depending on your passion and the cause you feel strongly about, NGOs offer a variety of career opportunities, from fighting a disease to working with animals to helping children who are living in poverty or abuse. Working for an NGO also enables you to travel the world if you so choose. The nature of the work—doing good and helping those in need—makes working in the NGO sector a fulfilling career path.

There is a misconception that all NGO work is volunteer based, which is not the case. Although careers in this field do tend to have lower salary ranges than similar jobs in the corporate world, it is definitely possible to earn a good wage working with an NGO. According to the website PayScale.com, as of February 2020, the average salary for a person working as a director or program manager is $60,000 per year.[1] Of course salaries vary with the work you do and the organization for which you are employed—these will be covered in more detail later in the book—but it is not true that you do not get a salary working for an NGO.

## *The Market Today*

How does the job market look for young people seeking to enter the NGO sector? Although the field is a competitive one, it is growing rapidly. According to *Fast Company*, the NGO sector is the third largest in the US job market (following retail and manufacturing). There are approximately 1.5 million nonprofit organizations operating in the United States alone,[2] with millions more around the world. In the United States, NGOs employ nearly 14 million people, which makes up about 10 percent of the workforce nationwide.[3] American NGOs focus on tackling issues such as the environment, women's rights, healthcare, politics, and economic development.

A career in the NGO sector offers a wide diversity of job roles,
as well as an equally diverse array of organizational missions. *Getty Images/laflor*

The future of the NGO sector is a positive one. In recent years, the NGO sector has increased in the United States and around the world. Looking at statistics of NGOs registered with the Internal Revenue Service, between 2005 and 2010 the number of NGOs increased 5.6 percent, and between 2005 and 2015 the increase was 10 percent.[4] And in terms of finances, accounting for not only NGOs but the nonprofit sector as a whole in the United States, between 2016 and 2018, total giving from individuals, foundations, and businesses equaled $10 billion—a 3 percent increase adjusting for inflation.

With so many already-existing NGOs in the United States and with so many new ones cropping up each year (later in this book you will see how you can launch your own), it is possible to find work within the sector wherever you live. Although many are based in major cities like New York and Washington, DC, there are opportunities for careers around the country, from rural to urban areas. And, of course, if you want to see the world, there is no better option than an NGO career.

"I went to Palestine where I worked for a few months as a volunteer with children in refugee camp. It was during this time that I perhaps learned the most, and without realizing, made the decisions that set out my career."—A. T., War Child and other NGOs

## What Does This Book Cover?

This book covers the following topics for all the aforementioned careers, as well as others:

- What kind of job best suits your personality and preference for working conditions, hours, educational requirements, work culture, and atmosphere, including the day-to-day activities involved in each job and what a typical day at work will look like
- How to form a career plan—starting now, wherever you are in your education—and how to start taking the steps that will best lead to success
- Educational requirements and opportunities and how to fulfill them
- Writing your résumé, interviewing, networking, and applying for jobs
- Resources for further information

Once you've read the book, you will be well on your way to understanding what kind of career you want, what you can expect from it, and how to go about planning and beginning your path. The book also includes stories of people who have made a difference by launching their own NGOs, acting on their own drive to see change in a particular issue. These are intended to inspire readers who may wonder what a difference a person can make by illustrating that, with enough energy and commitment, awareness and action can lead to improvement, regardless of the issue you want to tackle or the population you want to help see be better represented and respected in the world.

**INSPIRING STORIES**

While backpacking through India as a student, Adam Braun asked a child living on the street what he wanted most in life. When the child answered, "A pencil," Braun handed him one he'd been carrying in his backpack, and, as Braun later said in an interview, "I then saw the profound power and promise brought through something as small as a giving a pencil to just one child."[5] He continued for five years to travel the world, distributing pencils to children in need. He went on to found the organization Pencils of Promise, which has since been instrumental in the creation of more than 250 schools worldwide. Braun himself has been named to *Business Insider*'s "40 under 40," *Wired* magazine's "50 People Who Are Changing the World," and *Forbes*'s "30 under 30," and he was selected as one of the World Economic Forum's first ten Global Shapers.

## *Where Do You Start?*

All the jobs we cover in this book require at a minimum a high school degree or equivalent, such as a general educational development (GED) certificate, and some on-the-job training. Others require a four-year degree and even a master's degree—and the subjects you can follow will also vary. Law, communications, business, economics, politics, management, development, education, and human resources are just some of the areas of study that are applicable to a career in the NGO sector. Additional focus or experience is also useful to entering the field, depending on the type of NGO for which you want to work. All of this will be discussed later in the book.

A lot of choosing the right career for you will also depend on your personality and interests outside of work—such as whether you work better with people or independently; whether you want to be the boss or work for someone you admire; what you want your life to include outside of working hours—including hobbies and other activities that are important to you; and so on.

After high school, knowing how to choose and apply to vocational training such as an apprenticeship or a college program will be the next step in your path. The information in chapter 3 will help you navigate this important stage and know what questions to ask, how to best submit yourself as a candidate, and the right kinds of communication skills that are key to letting future employers or trainers understand who you are and what your potential is.

Thinking about the future and your profession is exciting and also a bit daunting. With this book, you will be on track for understanding and following the steps to get yourself on the way to a happy and successful future working in the NGO sector. Let's get started!

# 1

# *Why Choose a Career in the NGO Sector?*

*T*he fact that you picked this book off the shelves and are reading it means you have decided you are considering taking your interest in professional fields such as law, policy development, research, or communications and public relations and combining it with your passion for helping people and solving social and political issues.

That's a great start, but there's still a lot of decision making ahead. Choosing a career is a difficult task, but as we discuss in more detail in chapter 2, there are many methods and means of support to help you refine your career goal and hone in on a profession that will be satisfying and will fit you the best.

Of course, the first step is understanding what being part of a particular field—in this case the very broad and diverse NGO sector—actually entails and what possibilities it presents, and informing yourself about the future outlook of the profession. That is the emphasis of this chapter, which looks at defining the sector in general—its aims and what sets it apart from other types of organizations—and then looks more specifically at the different types of NGOs, their focus and aims, and the future outlook of the NGO sector in terms of employment opportunities and growth.

Working in the NGO sector, as mentioned in the introduction, gives you a chance to work together with people who share the same passion for solving a particular problem, be it animal rights or political issues, either nationally or, more often, globally. One step, then, is to really think about what matters to you, what you can imagine dedicating your work life to. If you are truly invested in the cause you are working for, you will be gifted with a strong sense of job satisfaction, be offered the chance to work among people who are interesting and care about similar issues, and be faced with lots of challenges that keep you learning and interested.

Of course, there are also some downsides to consider. While job satisfaction is high, salaries are often lower. And because most goals of an NGO are long-term, it can be difficult to measure in day-to-day terms whether your work is "succeeding." Equally, while an error you make in a corporate job might be financially costly, the stakes in the NGO world are often greater, risking doing more harm than good. So the pressure can be quite high. Additionally, working in the NGO sector, you will be dealing with a lot of bureaucratic "red tape," which can be frustrating and prevent you from making progress as quickly and efficiently as you'd like. The reliance on fundraising at an NGO can also be nerve-racking, as you must constantly consider where the money that supports your work will come from. The hours can also be long as you face the challenge of doing more work with fewer resources.

So as with any career, there are pros and cons, which we will discuss in this chapter. In balancing the good points and less attractive points of a career, you must ask yourself whether, in the end, the positive outweighs any negatives you may discover. This chapter will also help you decide whether a career in the NGO sector is actually the right choice for you. And if you decide it is, the next chapter will further offer suggestions for how to prepare your career path, including questions to ask yourself and resources to help you determine more specifically what kind of career related to the NGO sector suits you the very best.

## What Exactly Are NGOs?

As mentioned in the introduction, the NGO sector has been growing in recent years, with about 1.5 million organizations currently operating in the United States alone and millions more around the world. In total, this number is estimated to be a whopping 10 million.[1] This provides a lot of jobs and opportunities. In the United States, NGOs employ nearly 14 million people, which makes up about 10 percent of the workforce nationwide. Those are impressive statistics, but what exactly do NGOs do, and what impact do they have?

According to NGO.org, a website for NGOs associated with the United Nations, "a non-governmental organization (NGO) is any non-profit, voluntary citizens' group which is organized on a local, national or international level. Task-oriented and driven by people with a common interest, NGOs perform a variety of service and humanitarian functions, bring citizen concerns to Governments, advocate and monitor policies and encourage political participation through provision of information. Some are organized around specific issues, such as human rights, environment or health. They provide analysis and expertise, serve as early warning mechanisms, and help monitor and implement international agreements. Their relationship with offices and agencies of the United Nations system differs depending on their goals, their venue and the mandate of a particular institution."[2]

Working in with an NGO gives you an opportunity to work together with people who share your passion to make a difference. Getty Images/Jacob Ammentorp Lund

That's a bit of a mouthful, but in essence, an NGO is an organization independent from any government control that strives to make a difference in the world by addressing humanitarian, civil society issues to create solutions. The following sections outline NGOs by orientation and level of operation,[3] as well as some acronyms you will encounter that further define the reach or focus on a particular NGO.

## NGO TYPES BY ORIENTATION

The following describes NGOs as classified by orientation, which is basically level of involvement.

- *Charitable Orientation:* These NGOs involve a top-down approach in which the beneficiaries have little or limited participation, such as NGOs whose activities address distributing food, clothing, or vital medications to those without means and providing funding for infrastructure such as housing and schools. This may also include NGOs undertaking relief efforts following natural or man-made disasters.
- *Service Orientation:* These NGOs also engage in activities including the provision of health and family planning, but in this case the beneficiaries are expected to participate in the implementation of programs.
- *Participatory Orientation:* These NGOs engage in self-help projects in which the "locals" or beneficiaries get involved by contributing to funding the project or supplying necessary tools, land, and other materials, as well as labor.
- *Empowering Orientation:* These NGOs engage in projects intended to achieve self-reliance in the beneficiaries by helping them reach a better understanding of the social, political, and economic factors that underpin the issues that impact their lives negatively. This orientation involves the maximum participation on the part of beneficiaries, with the NGOs playing a facilitating role.

## NGO TYPES BY LEVEL OF OPERATIONS

The following describes NGOs as classified by level of operation:

- *Community-based Organizations (CBOs):* These initiatives arise from the benefiting community itself. They include things like sport clubs for kids, community organizations, and religious or educational organizations. These can be supported by national or international NGOs or can be independent—there is a wide variety.
- *Citywide Organizations:* This can include a variety of initiatives, such as Rotary or Lion's Club, chambers of commerce, and community

organizations or associations of such organizations. They can also focus on helping those in need.

- *National NGOs:* This includes national organizations such as the Red Cross, YMCA/YWCA, professional organizations, and so on. Some of these have state and city branches and support local NGOs.
- *International NGOs:* This is likely what most people think of when they hear the term "NGO." This includes organizations such as Save the Children, Oxfam, and CARE. Activities range from mainly funding local NGOs, institutions, and projects to implementing the projects themselves.

## NGO TYPES BY ACRONYM

You'll encounter lots of acronyms that describe NGO types, some of which may sound a little strange at first.

- BINGO: Business-friendly international NGOs, an example being the Red Cross
- ENGO: Environmental NGOs, such as Greenpeace and the World Wildlife Fund
- GONGO: Government-organized nongovernmental organizations, for example, the International Union for Conservation of Nature
- INGO: International NGOs, such as Oxfam
- QUANGO: Quasi-autonomous NGOs, which are something of a hybrid between a typical NGO and a government-funded organization; the International Organization for Standardization (ISO) is an example
- TANGO: Technical assistance NGOs, for example, the Em-power India Welfare Federation (EMPIWF)
- DONGO: Donor-organized NGOs, such as Sankalp India Foundation
- TNGO: Transnational NGOs, which are nongovernmental organizations that exist in more than one country
- GSO: Grassroots support organizations
- MANGO: Market advocacy NGOs, for example, Consulting for Social Good (GSG)

**WHAT IS THE DIFFERENCE BETWEEN AN NGO AND AN NPO?**

Although the two terms are sometimes used interchangeably, an NGO and a nonprofit organization (NPO) are not the same. Similar to an NGO, an NPO is an organization that works toward a goal that benefits society. But the two types of organizations differ in their scope, with NGOs focusing on broader international issues and NPOs working closer to home, often with cultural and social objectives but also including churches and alumni associations.

Unlike NGOs, which rely heavily on fundraising from individuals, initial funding for an NPO is raised by its members or trustees, individuals who have control over the property or assets and money of the organization. As a nonprofit, an NPO must apply surplus funds to promoting the organization's goals and paying its employers rather than distributing them to its members.

According to Top Nonprofits, the top five NPOs in the United States are:

1. Metropolitan Museum of Art
2. American Civil Liberties Union Foundation
3. Amnesty International USA
4. Planned Parenthood Federation of America
5. American Heart Association[4]

# A Short History of NGOs

The concept of a nongovernment organization first came to light with the creation in 1945 of the United Nations, which called for a role for organizations that would act as consultants but be separate from official government bodies. In 1950 the Economic and Social Council (ECOSOC) of the United Nations defined an NGO as "any international organization that is not founded by an international treaty."[5]

The term "nongovernmental organization" came into use with the establishment of the United Nations in 1945, with provisions in article 71 of chapter

10 of the United Nations Charter for a consultative role for organizations that are neither governments nor member states. The definition of international NGO (INGO) is first given in resolution 288 (X) of ECOSOC on February 27, 1950. The vital role of NGOs and other "major groups" in sustainable development was recognized in chapter 272 of agenda 21, leading to revised arrangements for consultative relationship between the United Nations and nongovernmental organizations.

## INSPIRING STORIES

Sister Anne Schenck is the founder of Furniture Bank, an organization that helps combat furniture poverty in Toronto, Ontario, Canada. Before launching this initiative, she worked as an educator. In 1989, she was sent to work at a refugee center in Toronto and was disheartened to see how little the families there had. She explains in an interview on the Furniture Bank website how she was inspired to start her own nonprofit to help families in need: "Back in 1989, I was asked by the congregation to open a refugee centre in Scarborough [now part of Toronto]. It was around that time that government reduced levels of funding for newcomers so they were literally moving into apartments with nothing. Interestingly, the family that inspired me into action wasn't even a family that came through that centre. I received word through a social agency that there was a lady who spoke no English who was basically, desperate for help. When I entered the house, I saw four kids—all under the age of five—sitting around a little 12" TV. I did a basic inventory of what she had in the kitchen: two plates, two forks, two tiny pots. I knew I couldn't cook myself dinner with what she had, let alone cook dinner for these four children. It was that moment that I said to myself that this shouldn't be happening in the city of Toronto. I was too busy running the refugee centre to do anything about it at that time but in that role, I was already collecting furniture and some household items. That's where it began."[6]

The United Nations—an international organization dedicated to preserving
international peace and security—was formed after World War II. *Getty Images/mizoula*

But although the term became official in a post–World War II environment, the origins of NGOs can be identified much earlier. As Peter Hall-Jones
writes in *Global Policy Forum*, the Anti-Slavery Society, which was in operation
starting from 1839, constitutes the first NGO, although perhaps not by name.[7]
Hall-Jones also cites other early NGOs that formed in postwar times, including
the Red Cross in the 1850s after the Franco-Austrian war, Save the Children
after World War I, and Oxfam and CARE after World War II.

## THE LARGEST NGOS IN THE UNITED STATES

Of the whopping 1.5 million NGOs in the United States, you may be wondering which
are the largest ones. Of course, such statistics vary depending on the criteria, according to the Public Interest Foundation, the following are the top ten NGOs operating in the US (Note: Some listed, such as the Mayo Clinic which ranks at the top of
the list, classify technically as non-profits:

1. *Mayo Clinic:* The Mayo Clinic is the largest NPO in the United States and is focused mainly on medical research. As with NPOs in general, all profits generated go toward upgrading services, training medical doctors, and supporting patient treatment.
2. *Feeding America (previously America's Second Harvest):* This organization focuses on eliminating hunger via a network of food banks. The values of the organization are respect, management and responsibility, cooperation, speed, service, integrity, and diversity.
3. *Catholic Charities USA:* One of the largest organizations in the United States, this charity helped more than 8 million people in 2008 alone. It is focused on helping those in need.
4. *Red Cross:* One of the best-known and oldest organizations in the United States and the world, the Red Cross is focused on organizing disaster relief activities around the world. It relies heavily on the support of volunteers and partners around the globe.
5. *AmeriCares:* This organization provides humanitarian and medical aid across the globe and also organizes relief activities following natural disasters such as floods and earthquakes. It focuses primarily on emergency response and healthcare recovery and also actively participates in support when epidemics break out.
6. *Feed the Children:* This organization focuses on addresses securing basic human needs for all, including needs such as food and nutrition, water and sanitation, education, and health. Its mission is "to create a world where no child goes to bed hungry."
7. *United Way:* The United Way is one of the largest organizations in the United States, with a worldwide reach. Its emphasis is on providing the tools, education, and health to enable people to reach their own potential. Beneficiaries are encouraged to participate.
8. *Salvation Army:* This is an organization of Christian churches and not technically an NGO, but its goal is to provide those in need with food and clothing.
9. *Gifts in Kind:* This is a charity of a different sort—and again, not technically classified as an NGO, but it made the list. It does not give direct money to people who need support but works with partners to provide support.
10. *YMCA:* Not just a fitness center (although also one), this organization works to create opportunities for learning and development through education and training programs.[8]

The term "civil society" is frequently used in association with the goals and function of NGOs. But what does this mean? In essence, it refers to a group of citizens who work together voluntarily to advance common goals. This includes advocacy organizations, public research organizations, organizations established to promote democracy and support human rights, and charities. It does not, however, include political parties at any level.

## The Pros and Cons of Working in the NGO Sector

As with any career—or with anything, for that matter—what one person perceives as a negative point is a positive one to someone else. If you are passionate about improving problematic circumstances and conditions in the world and are ready to commit yourself to working long hours and being confronted by difficult issues, such as children living in severe poverty, and if you are excited about the opportunity to work with a diverse group of people, then this could well be the right job for you. But if you want a more nine-to-five existence, like to see more short-term results (like celebrating a good fiscal quarter at a for-profit company), or have ambitions of making a list of the youngest billionaires (there's nothing wrong with that, so be honest with yourself), then perhaps this would *not* be a fulfilling career choice for you.

Although it's one thing to read about the pros and cons of a particular career, the best way to really get a feel for what a typical day is like on the job and what the challenges and rewards are is to talk to someone who is already working in the profession, or who has in the past.

Although each profession within the NGO sector is different, there are some generalizations that can be made when it comes to what is most challenging and most gratifying about the field.

Here are some general pros:

- You get to do what you love, focusing on issues you really care about and applying your skills to something you are deeply passionate about.
- The NGO sector tends to attract interesting, intelligent, hardworking, and compassionate people, so you will have colleagues to constantly be inspired by.
- The work is challenging on both a professional and a personal level. It will broaden your worldview and provide the opportunity to travel to parts of the world you may not have otherwise. It's a career that requires continuous learning.
- The feel-good factor: It's a field that enables you, in whatever capacity you work, to make a real difference in the world and help right wrongs.
- You will develop a deeper cultural understanding, working alongside or for people of different cultures and backgrounds.

And here are some general cons:

- Although job satisfaction is high, you can expect the salary to be relatively low compared to what you might earn doing the same type of work in a corporate environment.
- Success or the degree of "difference" you are making is difficult to measure in the short term. Contributing to real change in the world is a slow process, riddled with funding issues, red tape, resistance, and other unpredictable and uncontrollable factors.
- Due to many factors, there is a lot of burnout. Working at an NGO is not really a nine-to-five deal. Underfunding often forces employees to take on a lot of work without enough resources. The nature of the work—dealing with issues like poverty, hunger, and human rights abuses—can take its toll.
- It is a high-pressure field that requires an ability to manage stress well as well as to multitask and be flexible.
- It is an extremely competitive field. Breaking into it may require you to take on a role that is not the one you ultimately want to have. If you get that far, moving to a different role is possible, but may require time and patience.

"From a young age, I was struck by how injustice and inequality could exist. I couldn't understand how we could live in a world where children didn't have access to quality education or were dying from preventable diseases."—Olloriak Sawade, Oxfam

## How Healthy Is the NGO Job Market?

The NGO sector has been growing consistently over the last decades. Globalization has brought more issues to light, enabling the sharing of knowledge and awareness of the issues that impact people around the world and how even far-away issues eventually effect everybody. As mentioned in the introduction, the sector makes up the third largest in the US job market (following retail and manufacturing), and there are approximately 1.5 million nonprofit organizations operating in the United States alone.[9]

The future of NGOs depends a great deal on how many people want to create them, sustain them, and support them. And in that regard, the future looks bright. The millennial generation, according to *Forbes* magazine, is by nature connective, tech-savvy, and innovative. They are also entrepreneurial and have a social-change mindset, which ensures a passion for involvement and problem-solving thinking.[10]

### WHAT IS A MEDIAN INCOME?

Throughout your job search, you might hear the term "median income" used. What does it mean? Some people believe it's the same thing as average income, but that's not correct. While the median income and average income might sometimes be similar, they are calculated in different ways.

The true definition of median income is the income at which half of the workers earn more and the other half of workers earn less. If this is complicated, think of it this way: Suppose there are five employees in a company, each with varying skills and experience. Here are their salaries:

- $42,500
- $48,250
- $51,600
- $63,120
- $86,325

What is the median income? In this case, the median income is $51,600, because of the five total positions listed, it is in the middle. Two salaries are higher than $51,600, and two are lower.

The average income is simply the total of all salaries divided by the number of total jobs. In this case, the average income is $58,359.

Why does this matter? The median income is a more accurate way to measure the various incomes in a set because it's less likely to be influenced by extremely high or low numbers in the total group of salaries. For example, in our example of five incomes, the highest income ($86,325) is much higher than the other incomes, and therefore it makes the average income ($58,359) much higher than most incomes in the group. Therefore, if you base your income expectations on the average, you'll likely be disappointed to eventually learn that many of the incomes are below it.

But if you look at median income, you'll always know that half the people are above it and half are below it. That way, depending on your level of experience and training, you'll have a better estimate of where you'll end up on the salary spectrum.

While the Bureau of Labor Statistics (BLS) does provide salary data for general marketing, management, public relations, and other careers, it does not provide data specific to the NGO sector, and as noted, salaries are often lower at an NGO compared with a corporate for-profit business. What follows is salary information that is available online related to NGOs, based on data provided by Indeed.com. (BLS *does* list data for fundraiser jobs, which is listed below.)

## PROGRAM OFFICER

Program officers have an integral role within an NGO. They are tasked with overseeing program development, seeking grants and proposals, managing projects, and managing budgets. Annual wage: $89,961.[11]

## PROGRAM ASSISTANT

Program assistants provide administrative and logistical support for projects, initiatives, and programs within an NGO. This includes scheduling, arranging travel, and drafting contracts, budgets, and donor reports under the guidance of their manager. Average salary: $13.95 per hour.[12]

## FINANCIAL SPECIALIST

Financial specialists support the organization's budget planning and maintain the budget. Average salary: $66,205 per year.[13]

## POLICY MANAGER

Policy managers think strategically to create policy that will impact and influence initiatives within an NGO. Average salary: $85,077 per year. [14]

## PROGRAM DIRECTOR

Program directors are responsible for the daily operations of the NGO and planning to meet future goals. Average salary: $60,403.[15]

## PROGRAM COORDINATOR

Program coordinators are responsible for supporting developing strategies and programs, acting as a liaison between various actors within the organization. Average salary: $44,692.[16]

## FUNDRAISER

Fundraisers organize events and campaigns to raise money and other kinds of donations for an NCO. Average salary: $56,950.[17]

## *Am I Right for a Career in the NGO Sector?*

This is a tough question to answer, because really the answer can only come from you. But don't despair: There are plenty of resources both online and elsewhere that can help you find the answer by guiding you through the types of questions and considerations that will bring you to your conclusion. These are covered in more detail in chapter 2. But for now, let's look at the general demands and responsibilities of an NGO profession—as were mentioned previously in the section on pros and cons—and suggest some questions that may help you discover whether such a profession is a good match for your personality, interests, and the general lifestyle you want to keep in the future.

Of course, no job is going to match your personality or fit your every desire, especially when you are just starting out. There are, however, some aspects to a job that may be so unappealing or simply mismatched that you may decide to opt for something else, or equally, you may be so drawn to one feature of a job that any downsides are not that important.

Unlike some other fields, deciding to pursue a career in the NGO sector is a twofold thought process: You're considering not only whether you want to work with an NGO but also what role you wish to play within the sector. As mentioned earlier, NGOs require the same types of roles as other organizations —marketing, public relations, writers, researchers, financial wizards, marketing professionals—so one of your choices is which type of work you want to be doing in general. It would take volumes to list every job you can do at an NGO, so here let's focus on the second decision: Is the NGO world the right place for you career-wise?

One way to see if you may be cut out for a career with an NGO is to ask yourself the following questions:

- *Am I satisfied to have career-related goals with long-term benchmarks rather than more immediate success measures?*
  In the corporate world, targets and goals can be more easily measured than in an NGO, because of the nature of the work at an NGO and the various actors and influence that can impact a project.

- *When something goes wrong, can I think quickly on my feet to find a solution? Am I able to handle uncertainty and react effectively to it?*
  Unlike with for-profit companies, NGOs rely on donated funds, and therefore basic budget issues are a great challenge. Additionally, there is a lot of red tape, which forces some plans to have to shift and change. Flexibility is definitely required.
- *Am I able to handle stress well?*
  This is an important one. At an NGO, although the work can be very satisfying, it can also be enormously stressful and, frankly, emotionally charging. Although you will be working on solving problems, you will also be confronted with the full scope of the issues you are trying to resolve.
- *Can I consistently deal with people in a professional, friendly way?*
  Whether you are a manager, a volunteer, a volunteer manager, or serving in any other role, in the NGO world nobody is really acting alone. It's required that you be able to communicate well with people and equally be able to understand and respond to requests made of you.

## CONNECTING WITH PEOPLE THROUGH TRAINING

Lieke van Gompel.
*Lieke van Gompel*

Lieke van Gompel travels the world as a trainer and learning and development adviser for NGOs and humanitarian organizations. Before starting her freelance business, she worked for several years for NGOs such as Médecins sans Frontières/Doctors without Borders (MSF), both in the field (including in Afghanistan and the Central African Republic) and in the organization's headquarters. As she wanted to combine her passion for training and working for NGOs, in 2018 she decided to start her own freelance business, called Unlockyourpotential, providing leadership, management, and communication training.

## Why did you choose to become a trainer?

Whenever, during the early days of my career, I was sent to a training, I generally disliked it. I always had the feeling I was back in school again, with a one-dimensional exchange of information between the trainer and the participants. Then, when I was working for a Dutch NGO, SPARK, I ended up co-organizing a training in Ohrid (in North Macedonia) with an international training organization and participating myself. The training experience I had then and there was completely different from all I had experienced so far: The trainer was engaging, he was working with what we knew, he used a lot of visual props as opposed to boring PowerPoint presentations. I knew at that moment that I wanted to be a trainer, and engage with groups just like he did.

## What is a typical day on the job for you?

No day is the same! My assignments and clients are quite different. Some days I am developing training materials, some days I am traveling and delivering a training in another country, some days I am developing a strategic plan, and some days I just relax.

## What's the best part of your job?

The moment you are giving a training to a group of people, and you witness that moment where suddenly something "clicks" inside the participants, and they manage to tap into a hidden part of their own potential, and which they manage to bring up out in the open. This "aha" moment they experience. The connection with people is just fantastic.

## What's the worst or most challenging part of your job?

The irregularity of traveling, which is having a big impact on my health: the travels itself, which can be tiring, different nutrition, irregular days, etc. I can feel that sometimes I find it difficult to recharge sufficiently before going into the next assignment.

## What's the most surprising thing about your job?

It is only quite recent that organizations woke up to the importance of their human potential. Ten years ago, people were being laid off; now organizations are fighting to retain their employees. Unfortunately, though, many organizations still think that "just giving trainings" is enough to retain and develop people, but it requires a much more comprehensive approach. For example, the type of leadership and management being used in the organization, the values, transparency, excellent onboarding processes, and so much more.

## What kinds of qualities do you think one needs to be successful at this job?

I'd say two things are really key: a true interest in people, [that is], the ability to "read" them in order to find the key that will help them to discover their own potential. And the ability to show your own vulnerability. People will only open up, and be willing to learn, as you—as a trainer—show that you made many mistakes as well.

## How do you combat burnout?

This, I had to learn the hard way, unfortunately. During my time at MSF I did end up in a burnout, as I had never taken the time to really digest and recover from my time in Afghanistan. But now, what is keeping me sane and healthy is daily short meditations, a practice of gratefulness, and getting out for walks in the forest.

## What would you tell a young person who is thinking about becoming a trainer?

Realize that the connection that you will be able to establish with people is infinitely more important than showing up "as the expert." Many experts fall into the trap of wanting to talk about what they know instead of working with what the participants can contribute to the training. And be open to feedback. As a trainer you never stop learning. So ask for genuine feedback from the participants and from your cofacilitator.

---

# Summary

This chapter covered a lot of ground as far as looking more closely at the various types of professions and jobs that exist within the NGO sector. Because NGOs rely on the collaboration of so much talent from various backgrounds and skill sets, from fundraising to policy development, from campaigning and fundraising to communications and public relations, from volunteer management to research. Although this chapter was not exclusively about each job specifically, most of the information is relevant to the field as a whole.

In this chapter, we defined what an NGO is and the type of contribution such organizations make toward the goal of making the world a better place for all. We provided a brief history of NGOs and how they evolved, primarily after World War II but also earlier. Looking ahead at the future of NGOs, the growth that has occurred over the last decade is likely to continue, with the entrance of millennials and their principles and priorities, as well as the continuation of globalization, which makes the impact of the issues facing the world and the people in it more universal and highlights the benefit of creating solutions, making them a priority to everyone.

Here are some ideas to take away with you as you move on to the next chapter:

- The NGO sector is a broad one, in terms of the types of organizations that exist, the functions they perform, and the issues they confront.
- NGOs function as other businesses and organizations do, requiring many of the same roles. Salaries, however, are generally lower, and business models are also very different, as NGOs rely heavily on fundraising.
- Working at an NGO provides you an opportunity to work with interesting people who have similar passions and concerns, and offers you a career that is satisfying and also challenging. Still, there are some cons, and in this chapter we discsussed some questions to help you reflect and think more deeply about whether the pros outweigh the cons for you.

Assuming you are now more enthusiastic than ever about pursuing a career in the NGO sector, in the next chapter we will look more closely at how you can refine your choice to a more specific job. It offers tips and advice about how to find the role and work environment that will be most satisfying to you and what steps you can take—starting now!—toward reaching your future career goals.

# 2

# *Forming a Career Plan*

*I*t's not easy to choose a career, yet it is one of the most important decisions you will make in your life. There are simply so many options available, and it is easy to feel overwhelmed. Particularly if you have many passions and interests, it can be hard to narrow your options down. That you are reading this book means you have decided to investigate a career in the NGO sector, which means you have already discovered a passion for helping people, solving problems, contributing to societal well-being, and ongoing learning. But even within the NGO sector, there are many choices, including what role you want to pursue, what work environment you desire, and what type of work schedule best fits your lifestyle.

Working in the NGO sector is a broad goal, because so many careers exist within it. In many ways, the types of degrees and skill sets required for a job in a commercial company are the same as those required in the NGO sector. That's because the key difference between a job with an NGO and one in a for-profit company is the way the organizations operate and the type of projects they engage in. But both require experts in fields such as marketing, management, law, finance, and information technology, to name a few.

Before you can plan the path to a successful career in the NGO sector, it's helpful to develop an understanding of what role you want to have and in what environment you wish to work. Do you want to work in an office at a desk or do you see yourself out in the field around the world doing hands-on work? Do you want to engage with other people heavily or do you prefer to work with computers? Do you enjoy research? Do you want to work as an employee for one NGO or do you see yourself consulting with several organizations?

How much education would you like to pursue? Depending on your ultimate career goal, the steps to getting there differ. For a non-volunteer job with an NGO, you can expect that you will need a college degree, likely a bachelor's degree or higher. In some cases you will want to earn additional qualifications geared toward NGO work. The bachelor's degree you choose to pursue doesn't need to be particularly specific to an entry-level NGO career—but for more upper-level roles (such as program directors) or to pursue a career in with organizations with a specialized focus, you should consider a more specific degree, such as one in education, public health, or urban planning. You may also need to consider an advanced degree, such as a master's or a PhD. Increasingly, there are also degrees specifically focused on global development.

Deciding on a career means asking yourself big questions, but there are several tools and assessment tests that can help you determine what your personal strengths and aptitudes are and with which career fields and environments they best align. These tools guide you to think about important factors in choosing a career path, such as how you respond to pressure and how effectively you work and communicate with people—and how much you enjoy it.

This chapter explores the educational requirements for various careers within the NGO sector, as well as options for where to go for help when planning your path to the career you want. It offers advice on how to begin preparing for your career path at any age or stage in your education, including in high school.

## *Planning the Plan*

So where to begin? Before taking the leap and applying to college, there are other considerations and steps you can take to map out your plan for pursuing your career. Preparing your career plan begins with developing a clear understanding of what your actual career goal is.

Planning your career path means asking yourself questions that will help shape a clearer picture of what your long-term career goals are and what steps to take in order to achieve them. When considering these questions, it's important to prioritize your answers—when listing your skills, for example, put them in order of strongest to weakest. When considering questions relating to how you want to balance your career with the rest of your nonwork life, such as family and hobbies, really think about what your top priorities are and in what order.

## YOUR PASSIONS, ABILITIES, AND INTERESTS: IN JOB FORM

Think about how you've done at school and how things have worked out at any temporary or part-time jobs you've had so far. What are you really good at, in your opinion? What have other people told you you're good at? What are you not very good at right now, but you would like to become better at? What are you not very good at, and you're okay with not getting better at?

Now forget about work for a minute. In fact, forget about needing to ever have a job again. You won the lottery—congratulations! Now answer these questions: What are your favorite three ways to spend your time? For each one of those things, can you describe why you think you in particular are attracted to it? If you could get up tomorrow and do anything you wanted all day long, what would it be? These questions can be fun, but can also lead you to your true passions. The next step is to find the job that sparks your passions.

The following questions are helpful to think about deeply when planning your career path:

- Think about your interests outside of the work context. How do you like to spend your free time? What inspires you? What kind of people do you like to surround yourself with, and how do you best learn? What do you really love doing?
- Brainstorm a list of the various career choices within the NGO sector that you are interested in pursuing. Organize the list in order of which careers you find most appealing, and then list what it is about each that attracts you. This can be anything from work environment to geographical location to the degree to which you would work with other people in a particular role.
- Research information on each job on your career choices list. You can find job descriptions, salary indications, career outlook, salary, and educational requirements information online, for example.
- Consider your personality traits. How do you respond to stress and pressure? Do you consider yourself a strong communicator? Do you work well in teams or prefer to work independently? Do you consider yourself creative? Are you a good problem solver? How do you respond

to criticism? All of these are important to keep in mind to ensure you choose a career path that makes you happy and in which you can thrive.

- Although a career choice is obviously a huge factor in your future, it's important to consider what other factors feature in your vision of your ideal future. Think about how your career will fit in with the rest of your life, including whether you want to live in a big city or small town, if you want to travel extensively or live abroad, how much flexibility you want in your schedule, how much autonomy you want in your work, and what your ultimate career goal is.

- The NGO sector is a competitive one, particularly when you are starting out in your career. Because it requires so much commitment, it's important to think about how willing you are to put in long hours and perform what can be very demanding work.

- The NGO sector is generally a lower-paying one compared with the corporate environment. What are your pay expectations, now and in the future?

Posing these questions to yourself and thinking about them deeply and answering them honestly will help make your career goals clearer and guide you in knowing which steps you will need to take to get there.

Making a decision about what kind of career to pursue can be much simpler if you ask yourself some key questions. *Getty Images/Deagreez*

## OTHER USEFUL COURSES TO PURSUE

Although a degree in something directly related to your goal—development studies, law, finance, education, or healthcare, for example—will definitely help you get on track to the career of your dreams, there are other courses to consider that will help you succeed once your work life is launched in the NGO sector.

- *Communication courses.* Learning to be a strong communicator is an asset in any profession, but in the NGO sector it is particularly required. Knowing how to give and receive information and instructions clearly, being able to communicate with difficult people or in sensitive situations, and dealing with fundraising are all part of the job.
- *Foreign language.* Your work may involve international travel and working with people from various cultures. Having a second language is an asset for many reasons in life, but in this field it is particularly useful and often expected.
- *Business courses.* Understanding how to draft a project plan and manage a budget will be useful as you work on complicated projects and fund them.

## WHERE TO GO FOR HELP

The process of deciding on and planning a career path can seem daunting. In many ways, the range of choices of careers available today is a wonderful thing. It allows us to refine our career goals and customize them to our own lives and personalities. In other ways, though, too much choice can be extremely daunting and require a lot of soul-searching to navigate clearly.

Answering questions about your habits, characteristics, interests, and personality can be very challenging. Identifying and prioritizing all of your ambitions, interests, and passions can be overwhelming and complicated. It's not always easy to see ourselves objectively or see a way to achieve what matters most to us. But there are several resources and approaches to help guide you in drawing conclusions about these important questions.

- Take a career assessment test to help you answer questions about what career best suits you. There are several available online.

- Consult with a career or personal coach to help you refine your understanding of your goals and how to pursue them.
- Talk with professionals working in the job you are considering and ask them what they enjoy about their work, what they find the most challenging, and what path they followed to get there.
- Educate yourself as much as possible about the industry: what are the greatest challenges, what projects exist in a particular area or are directed at a particular problem that you are interested in.
- If possible, arrange to "job shadow" someone working in the field you are considering. This will enable you to experience in person what the atmosphere is like, what a typical workday entails, how coworkers interact with each other and with management, and how well you can see yourself thriving in that role and work culture.

## ONLINE RESOURCES TO HELP YOU PLAN YOUR PATH

The internet is an excellent source of advice and assessment tools that can help you find and figure out how to pursue your career path. Some of these tools focus on an individual's personality and aptitude, while others can help you identify and improve your skills to prepare for your career.

In addition to these sites, you can use the internet to find a career or life coach near you—many offer their services online as well. Job sites such as LinkedIn are a good place to search for people working in a profession you'd like to learn more about or to explore the types of jobs available in the NGO sector.

- At educations.com, you will find a career test designed to help you find the job of your dreams. Visit https://www.educations.com/career-test to take the test.
- The Princeton Review has created a career quiz that focuses on personal interests: https://www.princetonreview.com/quiz/career-quiz.
- The Bureau of Labor Statistics provides information, including quizzes and videos, to help students up to grade 12 explore various career paths. The site also provides general information on career prospects and salaries, for example, for various jobs in the NGO sector and other fields. Visit https://www.bls.gov to find these resources.

Young adults with disabilities can face additional challenges when planning a career path. DO-IT (Disabilities, Opportunities, Internetworking, and Technology) is an organization dedicated to promoting career and education inclusion for everyone. Its website contains a wealth of information and tools to help all young people plan a career path, including self-assessment tests and career exploration questionnaires.[1]

## *Making High School Count*

Once you have discovered your passion and have a fairly strong idea what type of career you want to pursue, you naturally want to start putting your career path plan into motion as quickly as you can. If you are a high school student, you may feel there isn't much you can do toward achieving your career goals—other than, of course, earning good grades and graduating. But there are actually many ways you can make your high school years count toward your career in the NGO sector before you have earned your high school diploma. This section will cover how you can use this period of your education and life to better prepare you for your career goal and to ensure you keep your passion alive while improving your skill set.

There's no reason to wait until you graduate from high school to start working toward your career goal. *Getty Images/ Vasyl Dolmatov*

## COURSES TO TAKE IN HIGH SCHOOL

Depending on your high school and what courses you have access to, there are many subjects that will help you prepare for a career in the NGO sector. Some of them may seem unrelated initially, but they will all help you prepare yourself and develop key skills.

- *Language arts.* Because team collaboration is the essence of a job in the NGO sector, ensuring you know how to communicate clearly and effectively—in both spoken and written language—will be key. It helps avoid unnecessary frustration, delays, financial and time costs, and errors if you can clearly convey and understand ideas.
- *Interpersonal communication/public speaking.* These courses will be an asset in any profession, including in the NGO sector. You will need to present ideas to your team, to donors, to the public—these will be very important skills to hone.
- *Business and economics.* As with any type of project-based field, or if you have the ambition to launch your own NGO, knowledge gained in business and economics classes will prepare you to make smarter planning and budget decisions.
- *Computer and technology classes.* Information technology plays a major part in many NGO projects, and having a basic knowledge of computers and technology will be an asset.
- *Science.* Classes in life science, agriculture-related courses, and health-related classes in particular will be of use.
- *Law courses.* People holding law degrees have a good chance at breaking into the NGO sector. Even if you do not wish to pursue a law degree in university, having knowledge of international law will be a benefit.

## GAINING WORK EXPERIENCE

The best way to learn anything is to do it. When it comes to preparing for a career in the NGO sector, there are several options for gaining real-world experience and getting a feel for whether you are choosing the career that is right for you.

The one big benefit of jobs in the NGO sector is you can make your own opportunities. Seek out local volunteer opportunities where you live. Even if you are not working for an actual NGO, participating in projects and programs or working for organizations that aim to address social issues will enable you to earn an enjoyable work experience, gain relevant knowledge, and add more substance to your résumé.

If you want to work with NGO focuses on animal rights, for example, you can consider working for your local chapter of the American Society for the Prevention of Cruelty to Animals (ASPCA) or volunteering for an animal shelter. If you want to work to eliminate poverty, you can volunteer at a homeless shelter or a place that serves meals to the hungry. You can even start your own initiative, such as a local food drive.

If your ambitions are farther afield, there are many travel abroad volunteer opportunities. These will come at your own expense, but the experience is both challenging and enormously satisfying, and it offers a real-world interaction with another country and culture and the issues facing the people in whatever region you visit.

## EXPERT ADVICE ON HOW TO START A SUCCESSFUL NGO

Ryan Libre is a photojournalist who has won awards for his work on the Kachin struggle for independence in Myanmar. He has also launched and worked with various NGOs. In an article on *Matador Network*, he offers advice on how to start an NGO in ten steps, which are summarized here.[2]

*Test the waters.* Libre does not wish to discourage the enthusiasm of those wanting to commit their lives to a cause, but enthusiasm alone will not lead to success as much as some mentorship will. He suggests, "There's no need to turn down the volume of your enthusiasm, but before starting your own NGO, consider joining one that does similar work for a while. If starting your own NGO really is right for you, the experience of working for an established NGO will only strengthen your resolve and direct your passion."

*Start on the right foot.* Libre says quite directly that being obsolete should be the ultimate goal of all NGOs. "You must constantly strive to work yourself out of a job," he writes. "Becoming obsolete works on two levels. In terms of your personal involvement, you should build the NGO to the point where it can function independently of your leadership. The long-term goal of your NGO should be to solve a problem and thereby become unnecessary."

*Clarify your goals.* Goals that are too lofty or vague or unachievable, such as "end world hunger," are unlikely to be successful. Libre recommends finding a niche, an issue you can actually impact positively.

*Make an action plan.* "A plan of action is your chance to make an NGO effective, address any potential negative impacts and make sure your NGO will attract donors and volunteers," he writes. "Make sure you are able to follow through with what you start. Think hard about your action plan. Hard work is important, but hard work without a good plan is a waste of time and money."

*Make a website.* Spread the word from the start, he suggests. It's never too early to gather interest, attract volunteers, and appear professional.

*Get in the know.* If there is a particular area you want to focus on in your work, make sure you are familiar with it and make solid local contacts. "Without local knowledge," he writes, "you can do more harm than good."

*Assess your NGO's financial needs.* "Money, when it does come, usually requires great amounts of paperwork and sometimes has strings attached," Libre writes. "The quality of the work an NGO does and the amount of its funding are often inversely related. That is to say, the NGOs with less money do better work per hour and dollar spent. The crucial point is to *minimize your NGO's need for money.*"

*Network, network, network.* Get to know organizations that do similar work with similar goals as yours.

*Find balance.* It's important to be realistic about how much time you can devote to your NGO without burning out. It's more effective to have life balance than to burn out in a few years.

*Reevaluate everything.* "Make sure your NGO is not becoming self-aggrandizing," he writes. "How much time, effort and money are being spent on the NGO itself? This is the biggest problem facing all organizations, non-governmental or otherwise." Be open to feedback and advice from outside your organization to ensure you are keeping aware.

If you are eager to begin volunteering and traveling, there are many volunteer abroad programs that offer you the chance to work as an English language teacher, healthcare worker, or animal caregiver—to name a few—around the globe. The site VolunteerForever.com provides a list of the top twenty such programs currently operating around the world.

## TIPS FROM THE EXPERTS: HOW TO LAUNCH A CAREER PATH

As mentioned throughout the book, breaking into and moving up within the NGO sector is certainly achievable and is a great career goal. However, in whatever capacity you wish to work, you are entering a competitive field, so standing out from others with the same ambitions as you have can be an additional challenge. The following advice comes from experts in the field of humanitarian aid—the focus of many NGOs—as shared in the *Guardian*.[3]

- Seek out whatever work experience you can find. Look for opportunities to volunteer—there are websites that offer this information. There are also opportunities online to volunteer remotely, including the United Nations Volunteers.
- Make yourself visible by commenting on articles or blogging about your own ideas. Attend conferences. This will help you keep abreast of current issues and debates in the field, shows your dedication and interest, and connects you with people doing the type of work you want to do yourself. These are all steps you can take before or during your studies.
- Don't focus only on the large organizations. Seek out local ones that may have ties with international organizations and, in any case, can offer you work experience.
- Stay persistent in moving into the type of work you really want to be doing. Although it is easier to break into the NGO sector if you are willing to be flexible about the exact role you will take on, it's important to keep networking, keep learning, and keep striving for your ultimate goal.

## *Educational Requirements*

Depending on the type of job you want to have in the NGO sector, you should consider degrees at various levels. Here, we will discuss the considerations to keep in mind when deciding what level of education is best for you to pursue. In chapter 3, we will outline in more detail the types of programs offered and the best schools to consider, should you want to pursue post–high school training and certification or an associate, bachelor's, or master's degree.

Generally speaking, if you wish to pursue a career in the NGO sector—as opposed to working as a volunteer—you should expect to need a bachelor's degree at minimum. While certification programs and associate's degrees may gain you more skills in relevant areas, given the competitive nature of the NGO sector, holding a bachelor's degree gives you the best shot at landing a professional job.

## *Formal Training Programs: Certification Programs, Community College, and University*

If you want to learn more about NGO work, international development, or humanitarian aid, for example, there are plenty of certification programs that can provide you with the training and knowledge to take part in humanitarian efforts organized by NGOs.

Check your local community college for relevant courses or take advantage of the internet and earn your certificate online—in some cases for free. Here are a few certification options that will help prepare you for work within the NGO sector:

- Peace Operations Training Institute (https://www.peaceopstraining .org): Provides the opportunity for participants to study peace support, humanitarian relief, and security operations conveniently online and at their own pace.

- DisasterReady (https://www.disasterready.org): Provides more than six hundred free online courses in humanitarian aid.
- Coursera (https://www.coursera.org): A portal of free courses that provides links to various humanitarian-related subjects at varying levels and from universities all over the world. Go to the start page and search for "humanitarian" or any other relevant topic.

Even if you intend to pursue or are pursuing a bachelor's degree or higher, additional certification—such as in cardiopulmonary resuscitation (CPR) or topics such as gender awareness—can give you additional knowledge and qualifications.

By following a certification program, you will get a foundation in development work and other related subjects. You will earn more about the profession and get a better feel for whether it is right for you. And because networking is so important in the NGO sector, getting to know instructors and professors and connecting with alumni of the program who are working in the field can help you establish contacts.

"No day is the same! My assignments and clients are quite different. Some days I am developing training materials, some days I am traveling and delivering a training in another country, some days I am developing a strategic plan, and some days I just relax."—Lieke van Gompel, freelance trainer at Unlockyourpotential

## WHY CHOOSE AN ASSOCIATE'S DEGREE?

A two-year degree—called an associate's degree—is sufficient to give you a knowledge base to begin your career and can serve as a basis should you decide to pursue a four-year degree later. Do keep in mind, though, that all jobs within the NGO sector are quite competitive. If you are prepared to put in the financial and time commitment to earn an associate's degree and are sure of the career goal you have set for yourself, consider earning a bachelor's instead. With so much competition out there, the more of an edge you can give yourself, the better your chances will be.

### Why Choose a Bachelor's Degree?

A bachelor's degree—which usually takes four years to obtain—is a requirement for most careers related to the NGO sector. In general, the higher education you pursue, the better your odds are to advance in your career, which means more opportunity and often more compensation.

The difference between an associate's and a bachelor's degree is, of course, the amount of time each takes to complete. To earn a bachelor's degree, a candidate must complete forty college credits, compared with twenty for an associate's. This translates to more courses completed and a deeper exploration of degree content, even though similar content is covered in both.

### Why Choose a Master's Degree?

A master's degree is an advanced degree that usually takes two years additional to complete after earning a bachelor's degree. A master's will offer you a chance to become more specialized and to build on the education and knowledge you gained while earning your bachelor's. A master's can be done directly after your bachelor's, although many people choose to work for a while in between in order to discover what type of master's degree is most relevant to their career and interests. Many people also earn their master's degree while working full- or part-time.

> Even when not required, a master's degree can help advance your career, give you an edge over the competition in the field, and give you more specific knowledge relating to your work in the NGO sector.

# COMMITTED TO WORKING FOR CHILDREN'S RIGHTS

A. T. (who would prefer her full name not be used) was born and raised in the UK. After studying for an MSc in social anthropology with development studies, and then MA in violence, conflict, and development, she moved to Palestine, where she volunteered as an English teacher with children living in refugee camps and Nablus. This formative experience has shaped her career in child rights for the last eighteen years. She has worked with several NGOs, conducting research, supporting child rights programming, and strengthening staff capacity in more than fifteen different countries, including Afghanistan, Sri Lanka, Palestine, Democratic Republic of the Congo, Syria, and Uganda. She now lives in the Netherlands with her husband and children.

## Why did you choose to become a professional in the NGO sector?

At the age of fifteen, I decided that I wasn't interested in working for a profit-making business, but wanted to support other people in the world. After leaving school, I studied for a degree in social anthropology with development studies at Edinburgh University, Scotland. During this time, I learned a lot about similarities between people in many different corners of the earth, as well as some of the differences, including significant inequalities. This motivated me further to work in international development, although I wasn't quite sure where to start.

Some people told me to "go to the field" and volunteer; others advised me to study further for a master's. I chose the latter and specialized my interest in conflict studies and development by studying at the School of Oriental and African Studies in London. Armed with knowledge but little hands-on experience, I went to Palestine, where I worked for a few months as a volunteer with children in a refugee camp. It was during this time that I perhaps learned the most, and without realizing, made the decisions that set out my career. I became interested in children's rights, and particularly in the experiences of children affected by armed conflict.

## What was your first NGO job, and how has your career progressed?

My first NGO job was still in Palestine—based in Ramallah, where I became responsible for monitoring child rights violations and reporting them to the UN, the media, and others. It was a difficult job—every day, seeing images and testimonials of children who had been killed or maimed, were unable to get to school safely, or who had been arrested and put in detention illegally and without trial. Yet it was very motivating and felt like I was raising awareness about many illegal practices that were taking place, preventing children from being children.

## What's the best part of your job?

Since this time, more than fifteen years ago, I have worked with many different child-focused NGOs around the world. My roles have included using child-friendly methodologies with children (and adults), to find out about their issues of greatest concern and the actions they want their communities and organizations to take to strengthen the realization of their rights. I might also help them, or organizations they are supported by, develop strategies to bring about changes that they desire.

Significant progress has been made to strengthen the realization of children's rights over the last thirty years. Even though huge progress needs to be made, more children get to school, increasing numbers of children get the medical care they need, many more children are able to influence decisions affecting them within families, schools, their wider community and at international levels, for example. Seeing this progress makes me very happy in my work.

Also, I love the variety of what I do. Each day, I might be working on a different project—looking at the impact of digital technologies on children, showing organizations how to make sure they prioritize children's best interests in every aspect of their work, or writing e-learning on children's rights. There is never a dull moment.

## What's the worst or most challenging part of your job?

The most challenging part of what I do is knowing that in many parts of the world, inequalities are growing, resulting in significant challenges for many children. Millions of girls still get married as children, for example. This can be frustrating, but it's important to focus on the small steps that you're contributing to.

## What's the most surprising thing about your job?

The most surprising thing about my job is how important it is. Every government has promised to prioritize children's rights in everything that it does relating to children, yet this is rarely the reality. NGOs spend a lot of time lobbying and advocating for governments and others with responsibilities to children to fulfill their obligations.

## What kinds of qualities do you think one needs to be successful at this job?

There are many ways to be involved in children's rights, so you can be successful in this field with a variety of skills. I wish I had done a qualification in human rights law—when I was younger I didn't even know such a thing existed. Even though I teach child rights law now, being able to claim a relevant legal qualification would immediately open more doors.

# *Summary*

This chapter covered a lot of ground in terms of how to break down the challenge of not only discovering what career within the NGO sector is right for you and in what environment, capacity, and work culture you want to work, but also how best to prepare yourself for achieving your career goal.

In this chapter, you learned about the broad range of roles that fall under the career umbrella of the NGO sector. In addition to the various careers that exist—from finance to on-the-ground aid worker—this chapter also pointed to many tools and methods that can help you navigate the confusing path to choosing a career that is right for you. It also addressed some of the specific training and educational options and requirements and expectations that will put you at a strong advantage in a competitive field, no matter what your current education level or age.

Use this chapter as a guideline for how to best discover what type of career will be the right fit for you and consider what steps you can already be taking to get there. Don't forget these important tips:

- Take time to carefully consider what kind of work environment you see yourself working in, and what kind of schedule, interaction with colleagues, work culture, and responsibilities you want to have.
- Most jobs within the NGO sector require the same skills as similar jobs in the commercial arena. But regardless of what degree you pursue, there are NGO-specific skills that will give you an edge, including IT knowledge, more than one language, and specialized knowledge such as in healthcare or education.
- Seek out as much work experience as you can, including making your own opportunities by launching your own initiatives. This is something you can do at any age or level of education.

# *Pursuing the Education Path*

*M*aking decisions about your educational path can be just as daunting as choosing a career path. It is a decision that not only demands understanding what kind of education or training is required for the career you want, but also what kind of school or college you want to attend. There is a lot to consider no matter what area of study you want to pursue, and depending on the type of job you want to have within the NGO sector.

Now that you've gotten an overview of the different degree and certificate options that can prepare you for your future career, this chapter will dig more deeply into how to best choose the right type of study for you. Even if you are years away from earning your high school diploma or equivalent, it's never too soon to start weighing your options, thinking about the application process, and, of course, taking time to really consider what kind of educational track and environment will suit you best.

Some people choose to start their careers right away after graduating with a high school diploma or equivalent. For some jobs, mostly volunteer or entry-level jobs within the NGO sector, this is possible. Not everyone wants to take time to go to college or pursue other forms of academic-based training. But if you are interested in following the educational path, this chapter will help you navigate the process of deciding on the type of institution you would most thrive in, determining what type of degree you want to earn, and looking into costs and how to find help in meeting them.

According to the National Center for Education Statistics (NCES), which is part of the US Department of Education, six years after entering college for an undergraduate degree, only 60 percent of students have graduated.[1] Barely half of those students will graduate from college in their lifetime.[2]

By the same token, it's never been more important to get your degree. College graduates with a bachelor's degree typically earn 66 percent more than those with only a high school diploma and are also far less likely to face unemployment. Also, over the course of a lifetime, the average worker with a bachelor's degree will earn approximately $1 million more than a worker without a postsecondary education.[3]

The chapter will also give you advice on the application process, how to prepare for any entrance exams you may need to take (such as the SAT or ACT), and how to communicate your passion, ambition, and personal experience in a personal statement. When you've completed this chapter, you should have a good sense of what kind of post–high school education is right for you and how to ensure you have the best chance of being accepted at the institution of your choice.

"I also knew that the voluntary sector really values all-rounders, people that can adapt, transfer their skills and undertake a range of tasks and just get stuck in to get the job done. This really excited me as it meant there would be great opportunities for me to develop a wide range of skills sets which would benefit my career in the long term."—Charlene Overend, Head of Partnerships, Purple

## Finding a Program or School That Fits Your Personality

Before we get into the details of good schools for each profession, it's a good idea for you to take some time to consider what type of school will be best for you. Just as with your future work environment, understanding how you best learn, what type of atmosphere best fits your personality, and how and where you are most likely to succeed will play a major part in how happy you will be with your choice. This section will provide some thinking points to help you refine what kind of school or program is the best fit for you.

Note that this list does not assume you intend to attend a four-year college program or complete a certification program—some of the questions may therefore be more relevant to you, depending on the path of study you mean to follow.

According to the US Department of Education, as many as 32 percent of college students transfer colleges during the course of their educational career.[4] This is to say that the decision you initially make is not set in stone. Do your best to make a good choice, but remember that you can change your mind, your major, and even your campus. Many students do it and go on to have great experiences and earn great degrees.

If nothing else, answering questions like the following ones can help you narrow your search and focus on a smaller sampling of choices. Write your answers to these questions down somewhere where you can refer to them often, such as in the Notes app on your phone:

- *Size:* Does the size of the school matter to you? Colleges and universities range from sizes of five hundred or fewer students to twenty-five thousand students. If you are considering college or university, think about what size classes you would like and what the right instructor-to-student ratio is for you.
- *Community location:* Would you prefer to be in a rural area, a small town, a suburban area, or a large city? How important is the location of the school in the larger world to you? Is the flexibility of an online degree or certification program attractive to you, or do you prefer more on-site, hands-on instruction?
- *Length of study:* How many months or years do you want to put into your education before you start working professionally?
- *Housing options:* If applicable, what kind of housing would you prefer? Dorms, off-campus apartments, and private homes are all common options.
- *Student body:* How would you like the student body to look? Think about coed versus all-male and all-female settings, as well as the makeup

of the student body in terms of diversity, how many students are part-time versus full-time, and percentage of commuter students.

- *Academic environment:* Consider which majors are offered and at which degree levels. Research the student-faculty ratio. Are the classes taught often by actual professors or more often by the teaching assistants? Find out how many internships the school typically provides to students. Are independent study or study abroad programs available in your area of interest?
- *Financial aid availability/cost:* Does the school provide ample opportunities for scholarships, grants, work-study programs, and the like? Does cost play a role in your options? (For most people, it does.)
- *Support services:* Investigate the strength of school's academic and career placement counseling services.
- *Social activities and athletics:* Does the school offer clubs that you are interested in? Which sports are offered? Are scholarships available?
- *Specialized programs:* Does the school offer honors programs or programs for veterans or students with disabilities or special needs?

Not all of these questions are going to be important to you, and that's fine. Be sure to make note of aspects that don't matter so much to you, such as size or location. You might change your mind as you go to visit colleges, but it's important to make note of what you're feeling to begin with.

*U.S. News & World Report* puts it best when it reports that the college that fits you best is one that:

- Offers a degree that matches your interests and needs
- Provides a style of instruction that matches the way you like to learn
- Provides a level of academic rigor to match your aptitude and preparation
- Offers a community that feels like home to you
- Values you for what you do well[5]

## MAKE THE MOST OF CAMPUS VISITS

If it's at all practical and feasible, you should visit the campuses of all the schools you're considering. To get a real feel for any college or university, you need to walk around the campus, spend some time in the common areas where students hang out, and sit in on a few classes. You can also sign up for campus tours, which are typically given by current students. This is another good way to see the campus and ask questions of someone who knows. Be sure to visit the specific school or building that houses your possible major as well. The website and brochures won't be able to convey that intangible feeling you'll get from a visit.

Make a list of questions that are important to you before you visit. In addition to the questions listed in the section "Finding a College That Fits Your Personality," consider these questions as well:

- What is the makeup of the current freshman class? Is the campus diverse?
- What is the meal plan like? What are the food options?
- Where do most of the students hang out between classes? (Be sure to visit this area.)
- How long does it take to walk from one end of the campus to the other?
- What types of transportation are available for students? Does campus security provide escorts to cars, dorms, and so on at night?

In order to be ready for your visit and make the most of it, consider these tips and words of advice:

- Be sure to do some research. At the very least, spend some time on the college website. Make sure your questions aren't addressed adequately there first.
- Make a list of questions.
- Arrange to meet with a professor in your area of interest or to visit the specific school.
- Be prepared to answer questions about yourself and why you are interested in this school.
- Dress in neat, clean, and casual clothes. Avoid overly wrinkled clothing or anything with stains.
- Listen and take notes.

- Don't interrupt.
- Be positive and energetic.
- Make eye contact when someone speaks directly to you.
- Ask questions.
- Thank people for their time.

Finally, be sure to send thank-you notes or e-mails after the visit is over. Remind recipients when you visited the campus and thank them for their time.

Hopefully, this section has impressed upon you the importance of finding the right fit for your chosen learning institution. Take some time to paint a mental picture about the kind of university or school setting that will best complement your needs. Then read on for specifics about each degree.

In the academic world, accreditation matters, and this is something you should consider when choosing a school. Accreditation is basically a seal of approval that ensures prospective students the institution will provide a quality education that is worth the investment and will help graduates reach their career goals. Future employers will want to see that the program you completed has such a seal of quality, so it's something to keep in mind when choosing a school.

## Determining Your Education Plan

As mentioned earlier, there are many options when it comes to pursuing further education after high school. These include vocational schools, two-year community colleges, and four-year colleges. This section will help you select the track that is most suited to you.

## CONSIDERING A GAP YEAR

Taking a year off between high school and college, often called a gap year, is normal, perfectly acceptable, and almost required in many countries around the world, and it is becoming increasingly acceptable in the United States as well. Because the cost of college has gone up dramatically, it literally pays for you to know going in what you want to study, and a gap year—well spent—can do lots to help you answer that question. It can also give you an opportunity to explore different types of NGO-sector-related jobs to help you find a deeper sense of what you'd like to study when your gap year has ended.

Some great ways to spend your gap year include joining the Peace Corps or another organization that offers opportunities for work experience. But even if the experience has nothing to do directly with humanitarian work, a gap year can help you see things from a new perspective. Consider enrolling in a mountaineering program or other gap year–styled program, backpacking across Europe or other countries on the cheap (be safe and bring a friend), finding a volunteer organization that furthers a cause you believe in or that complements your career aspirations, joining a Road Scholar program (see https://www.roadscholar.org), teaching English in another country (see https://www.gooverseas.com/blog/best-countries-for-seniors-to-teach-english-abroad for more information), or working to earn money for college!

Many students will find that they get much more out of college when they have a year to mature and to experience the real world. The American Gap Year Association reports from its alumni surveys that students who take a gap year show increased civic engagement, improved college graduation rates, and higher GPAs in college.

See the association's website at https://gapyearassociation.org/ for lots of advice and resources if you're considering this potentially life-altering experience.

Whether you are opting for a certificate program or a two-year or four-year degree, you will find you have a choice of many institutes and schools offering a variety of programs at different costs and durations (in the case of certificate programs, twelve to eighteen months is usually the average for full-time participants to complete the required course load). Because of this, it is important to narrow down your options and compare them closely.

It's a good idea to select roughly five to ten schools in a realistic location (for you) that offer the degree or certification you want to earn. If you are considering online programs, include these in your list. Of course, not every school near you or that you have an initial interest in will grant the degree you want, so narrow your choices accordingly. With that said, consider attending a university in your resident state, if possible, which will save you lots of money if you attend a public school. Private institutions don't typically discount resident student tuition costs.

Be sure you research the basic GPA and SAT or ACT requirements of each school as well. Although some community colleges do not require standardized tests for the application process, others do.

If you are planning to apply to a college or program that requires the ACT or SAT, advisers recommend that you take both tests during your junior year (spring at the latest). You can retake these tests and use your highest score, so be sure to leave time for a retake early in your senior year if needed. You want your best score to be available to all the schools you're applying to by January of your senior year, which will also enable them to be considered with any scholarship applications. Keep in mind that these are general timelines—be sure to check the exact deadlines and calendars of the schools to which you're applying!

Once you have found five to ten schools in a realistic location that offer the degree or certification in question, spend some time on their websites studying the requirements for admissions. Important factors weighing on your decision about what schools to apply to should include whether or not you meet the requirements, your chances of getting in (but shoot high!), tuition costs and availability of scholarships and grants, location, and the school's reputation and licensure/graduation rates.

## ALL ABOUT THE COMMON APP

The Common Application form is a single, detailed application form that is accepted by more than nine hundred colleges and universities in the United States. Instead of filling out a different application form for every school you want to apply to, you fill out one form and have it sent to all the schools you're interested in. The Common App itself is free, and most schools don't charge for submitting it.

If you don't want to use the Common App for some reason, most colleges will also let you apply using a form on their website. There are a few institutions that require you to apply through their sites and other highly regarded institutions that only accept the Common App. Be sure you know what is preferred by the schools that interest you.

The Common App website (https://www.commonapp.org) has a lot of useful information, including tips for first-time applicants and for transfer students.

Most colleges and universities list the average stats for the last class accepted to the program, which will give you a sense of your chances of acceptance.

The order of these characteristics will depend on your grades and test scores, your financial resources, your work experience, and other personal factors. Taking everything into account, you should be able to narrow your list down to the schools that best match your educational or professional goals as well as your resources and other factors such as location and duration of study.

## *Schools to Consider When Pursuing a Career in the NGO Sector*

Some schools and programs have stronger reputations than others. Although you can certainly have a successful and satisfying career and experience without going to the number one school in your field of study, it is a good idea to shop around, to compare different schools and get a sense of what they offer and what features of each are the most—or least—important to you.

Remember that what is great for one person may not be as great for someone else. What might be a perfect school for you might be too difficult, too expensive, or not rigorous enough for someone else. Keep in mind the advice of the previous sections when deciding what you really need in a school.

Also, bear in mind there are different degree programs you can follow in order to land a career with an NGO. So while programs designed specifically for humanitarian aid and global development careers exist, for example, you don't necessarily have to attend one to prepare for a future in the field.

## AN NGO FOUNDER'S FIRST YEAR: TWELVE VALUABLE LESSONS

Anu Prasad is the founder-director of India Leaders for Social Sector (ILSS) Nurturing Leaders for a Better Tomorrow. ILSS aims at creating a learning and leadership development organization that will help build leadership capacity for India's social sector. She offers twelve lessons she learned in her first year as an NGO founder at SheThePeople.[6]

*Just do it.* Prasad advises young entrepreneurs to dive straight in and let the idea and start-up evolve rather than trying to nail everything down before you take the first step.

*Be flexible.* Don't be too rigid about your business plan or you will close yourself off from other opportunities that can further your cause.

*Yours is to ask why.* Always be curious, always be questioning, always be open to the ideas of others from any sector that may enhance or inform your own.

*Stay humble.* Relationship building is key in the NGO sector. Be genuine and have honest conversations to nourish trust in these relationships.

*Be hands-on.* Humility aside, this is still your baby. Stay close and stay involved and look after it, staying energized and watching every step.

*Build your team.* Being hands-on does not mean doing it all yourself. That will surely lead to burnout and failure. Form a team of true partners rather than mere employees. And allow them space to development themselves, which will only help your organization's success.

*Find your champions.* It's lonely at the top, as they say. Find people who can provide you support but also offer you honest, constructive feedback.

*Get a thicker skin.* This is particularly true, Prasad writes, for female entrepreneurs. "You will come under more scrutiny and skepticism than men," she writes, "so the sooner you develop the art of separating honest feedback from plain negativity and cynicism, the easier it will be for you to stay mission-focused and happy with what you do."

*Value your relationships.* Invest time into your relationships—be they funders or partners—to ensure they believe in your business and are genuinely rooting for your success.

*Money matters.* Don't be afraid to discuss money. And don't get caught up getting funding for the sake of doing more things—"You could instead land up doing too many things that don't necessarily help you achieve the impact you were really keen to achieve," Prasad warns.

*Communicate.* Never miss the opportunity to speak up and speak out. Prasad emphasizes that this is particularly important for women, who she believes tend to underplay their achievements.

*Keep learning.* Have a continuously learning and open mind. Always seek out a chance to read and learn and discuss.

In this chapter, we will focus on those programs that are geared more toward NGO-sector careers, rather than, for example, examining various marketing, business, pre-law, or pre-med degree programs, even though these are equally relevant fields of study when looking at undergraduate degree options.

## GREAT BACHELOR'S PROGRAMS TO LAUNCH YOUR NGO CAREER

As mentioned earlier in this book, most undergraduate degrees will provide you an education and background that is applicable to a career in the NGO sector. If you are considering a master's degree, you will probably want to look at something more specialized, which we will cover in the next section. Here we list some of the best majors to consider during your undergraduate or bachelor's degree studies and some of the best schools offering these degrees.

- *Bachelor's in social work.* Top schools include the University of Georgia and North Carolina State University.
- *Bachelor's in business administration.* Top schools include the University of Pennsylvania and the University of California, Davis.
- *Bachelor's in sociology.* Top schools include the University of California, Berkeley.
- *Bachelor's in anthropology.* Top schools include the University of California, Berkeley and the University of California, Los Angeles.
- *Bachelor's in pre-law.* Top schools include Cornell University and Kansas State University.
- *Bachelor's in education.* Top schools include Arizona State University and City University of Seattle.
- *Bachelor's in global development.* Top schools include Stanford University and the University of California, Berkeley.
- *Bachelor's in environmental sciences.* Top schools include Washington and Jefferson College and the University of Mary Washington.
- *Bachelor's in agricultural sciences.* Top schools include University of Hawaii, Hilo and Northern Arizona University.
- *Bachelor's in pre-med.* Top schools include the University of Arizona and the University of Alabama.

## ONLINE DEGREES TO CONSIDER IN HUMANITARIAN AID

It is increasingly possible to earn a broad range of degrees without having to relocate or face the additional expense of campus living. Online degrees that are of equal value to their on-campus counterparts offer you the flexibility of location and often schedule, so you can earn your degree while continuing to work, for example.

The following are ten degree programs you can follow online that are definitely relevant to a future with an NGO and will appeal to you as a person who is committed to a career that enables you to help others and conquer problems. This list was compiled by BestDegreePrograms.org.

The degree programs listed here are also majors you could consider studying on campus, not just online.

10. Bachelor's in Political Science

Knowledge of law and politics will provide you with the background and skills to work for a global organization. In the course of earning this degree, you will have the opportunity to study subjects such as environmental politics, international relations, and comparative politics. You can also opt for a specialization, such as humanitarian relief. Schools offering this degree online include Arizona State University and the University of Massachusetts.

9. Bachelor's in Sociology

A degree in sociology will give you a background in such topics as cultural and social diversity, global social processes, and political science and government. You will gain knowledge in understanding societies and ways to bring about social change. Online sociology students have opportunities to join online sociology clubs and organizations. A sociology degree is one of the best online degrees for humanitarians and those interested working for nonprofits or NGOs. Schools offering this degree online include Ashford University and Southern New Hampshire University.

8. Bachelor's in Economics

This degree provides a solid foundation for anyone interested in working as a humanitarian. An online economics degree program with a humanitarian focus will include courses on international economics, labor economics, and social and behavioral sciences. This highly specialized social science program will give you the educational background to prepare you for a career as a nonprofit administrator, manager, or economic expert. Schools offering this degree online include Pennsylvania State World Campus and Utah State University.

7. Master's in International Relations

A master's in international relations is a good degree to consider if you are looking to continue your education beyond a bachelor's degree. If you are interested in a career in foreign policy, diplomatic relations, or international affairs, this degree is virtually a necessity. You will gain expert communication skills and hone your critical thinking abilities. With this degree, you can choose to further specialize, for example, in nonprofit management, international development, or global health. Schools offering this degree online include St. Mary's University, Texas and the University of North Georgia.

6. Bachelor's in Women's Studies

If you are passionate about women's rights, this is a good degree to consider. A degree in women's studies will cover a lot of ground, from education to health to law. You will study such topics as feminist research methods, women and immigration, and transnational feminism. NGOs focused on women's issues around the world are interested in students with such a background. Schools offering this degree online include Armstrong State University and New Mexico State University.

5. Bachelor's in Spanish

A second (or more) language is a strong asset in any career, but particularly within the NGO sector. Working with and for people of different cultures is a challenge, and having a solid background in another culture and language will eliminate some of the obstacles that face NGOs. You will not only study the language, but the history, politics, and culture of the regions where the language is spoken, giving you a broader understanding of the region in which you may be working, which will aid in your success. Schools offering this degree online include Mercy College and National University.

4. Bachelor's in Social Work

This is one of the best online degrees you can choose for a career in the NGO or humanitarian field. You will take courses in such subjects as ethical considerations in social work, human behavior and the social environment, and social welfare policy. Field work opportunities and research projects enable you to apply the theory you have learned to real-world situations. Schools offering this degree online include Brescia University and Wayne State University.

3. Master's in Human Services

This degree will give you the opportunity to advance your studies while diving more deeply into theory and its application to a humanitarian career. You will hone the ability to assess funding and operating processes of NGOs and learn vital project management skills. You will have the chance to study such courses as ethics for human services, human services administration, nonprofit administration, and social and cultural diversity. Schools offering this degree online include Bellevue University and Northeastern University.

2. Master's in Public Health

Public health is a major issue, nationally and worldwide, and an educational background in this very relevant and urgent subject will help set you on your way to a career with an NGO. During your studies, you will take courses in subjects such as health policy and ethics, public health service administration, and social contexts of healthcare. The degree is focused on knowledge that can be applied to humanitarian efforts, and most can be completed entirely online without on-campus or in-clinic residencies. Schools offering this degree online include Creighton University and the University of South Florida.

1. Master's in Human Rights

This is an excellent degree to consider for anyone interested in making a real, lasting difference in society. The degree will prepare you for a career as a global leader, innovator, and advocacy specialist for human rights everywhere. You will follow coursework in subjects including economic development, foreign policy, and issues in human dignity. You can gain practical experience by completing internships and participating in fieldwork positions around globe. Schools offering this degree online include the University of Denver and the University of Connecticut.

## GREAT MASTER'S PROGRAMS TO LAUNCH YOUR NGO CAREER

Continuing your education and refining your focus with a master's degree is a very sensible if not always necessary plan if you want to pursue a higher-level management or director role within the NGO sector. A master's can be pursued directly upon completing a bachelor's degree, although many people prefer to have a little more time working professionally in between degrees in order to get a deeper sense of the career they want to have and the type of degree required to meet their goals. A master's can also be completed while you are working full time, as many are offered part time or as online programs.

Here are the top ten master's programs in the United States to consider for a career within the NGO sector, as well as some of the top schools offering such degrees.

- *Master's in public policy or administration.* Top schools include Harvard University and the University of California, Berkeley.
- *Master's in business administration.* Top schools include Harvard University and the University of Chicago.
- *Master's in public health.* Top schools include Harvard University and John Hopkins University.
- *Master's in engineering.* Top schools include Arizona State University and the University of California, Davis.
- *Master's in education.* Top schools include Harvard University and the University of Pennsylvania.
- *Master's in anthropology.* Top schools include Harvard University and the University of California, Berkeley.
- *Master's in environmental sciences.* Top schools include Columbia University and the University of Colorado, Boulder.
- *Master's in agricultural sciences.* Top schools include Duke University and Cornell University.
- *Master's in nutrition/food science.* Top schools include Michigan State University and Purdue University.
- *Master of laws degree.* Top schools include Columbia University and New York University.

# *What's It Going to Cost You?*

So, the bottom line—what will your education end up costing you? Of course, that depends on many factors, including the type and length of degree or certification, where you attend (in-state or not, private or public institution), how much in scholarships or financial aid you're able to obtain, your family or personal income, and many other factors.

Generally speaking, there is about a 3 percent annual increase in tuition and associated costs to attend college. In other words, if you are expecting to attend college two years after this data was collected, you need to add approximately 6 percent to these numbers. Keep in mind that this assumes no financial aid or scholarships of any kind.

School can be an expensive investment, but there are many ways to get help paying for your education. *Getty Images/MonthiraYodtiwong*

## NOT ALL FINANCIAL AID IS CREATED EQUAL

Educational institutions tend to define financial aid as any scholarship, grant, loan, or paid employment that assists students to pay their college expenses. Notice that financial aid includes both *money you have to pay back* and *money you don't have to pay back*. That's a big difference!

Do Not Have to Be Repaid

- Scholarships
- Grants
- Work-study

Have to Be Repaid *with Interest*

- Federal government loans
- Private loans
- Institutional loans

## FINANCIAL AID TIPS

- Some colleges/universities will offer tuition discounts to encourage students to attend—so tuition costs can be lower than they first appear.
- Apply for financial aid during your senior year of high school. The sooner you apply, the better your chances.
- Compare offers from different schools. One school may be able to match or improve on another school's financial aid offer.
- Keep your grades up. A good GPA helps a lot when it comes to merit scholarships and grants.
- You have to reapply for financial aid every year, so you'll be filling out that FAFSA form again!
- Look for ways that loans might be deferred or forgiven. Service commitment programs are a way to use service to pay back loans.

## WRITING A GREAT PERSONAL STATEMENT FOR ADMISSION

The personal statement you include with your application to college is extremely important, especially when your GPA and SAT/ACT scores are on the border of what is typically accepted. Write something that is thoughtful and conveys your understanding of the profession you are interested in as well as your desire to practice in the field. Why are you uniquely qualified? Why are you a good fit for the university? These essays should be highly personal (the "personal" in personal statement). Will the admissions professionals who read it, along with those of hundreds of other applicants, come away with a snapshot of who you really are and what you are passionate about?

Look online for some examples of good essays, which will give you a feel for what works. Be sure to check your specific school for length guidelines, format requirements, and any other guidelines you are expected to follow. And of course, be sure to proofread it several times and ask a professional (such as your school writing center or your local library services) to proofread it as well.

## *Financial Aid: Finding Money for Education*

Finding the money to attend college, whether it is a two- or four-year degree, an online program, or a vocational career college, can seem overwhelming. But you can do it if you have a plan before you actually start applying to college. If you get into your top-choice university, don't let the sticker price turn you away. Financial aid can come from many different sources and is available to cover all the different kinds of costs you'll encounter during your years in college, including tuition, fees, books, housing, and food.

The good news is that universities more often offer incentive or tuition discount aid to encourage students to attend. The market is often more competitive in the favor of the student, and colleges and universities are responding by offering more generous aid packages to a wider range of students than they used to. Here are some basic tips and pointers about the financial aid process:

- You apply for financial aid during your senior year. You must fill out the Free Application for Federal Student Aid (FAFSA) form, which can be filed starting October 1 of your senior year until June of the year you graduate.[7] Because the amount of available aid is limited, it's best to apply as soon as you possibly can. See https://studentaid.ed.gov/sa/fafsa to get started.
- Be sure to compare and contrast deals you get at different schools. There is room to negotiate with universities. The first offer for aid may not be the best you'll get.
- Wait until you receive all offers from your top schools and then use this information to negotiate with your top choice to see if they will match or beat the best aid package you received.
- To be eligible to keep and maintain your financial aid package, you must meet certain grade/GPA requirements. Be sure you are very clear on these academic expectations and keep up with them.
- You must reapply for federal aid every year.

Watch out for scholarship scams! You should never be asked to pay to submit the FAFSA form ("free" is in its name) or be required to pay a lot to find appropriate aid and scholarships. These are free services. If an organization promises you'll get aid or that you have to "act now or miss out," these are both warning signs of a less-than-reputable organization.

Also, be careful with your personal information to avoid identity theft. Simple things like closing and exiting your browser after visiting sites where you entered personal information goes a long way. Don't share your student aid ID number with anyone, either.

It's important to understand the different forms of financial aid that are available to you. That way, you'll know how to apply for different kinds and get the best financial aid package that fits your needs and strengths. The two main categories that financial aid falls under is gift aid, which doesn't have to be repaid, and self-help aid, which includes both loans that must be repaid and work-study funds that are earned. The next sections cover the various types of financial aid that fit into these areas.

## GRANTS

Grants typically are awarded to students who have financial needs but can also be used in the areas of athletics, academics, demographics, veteran support, and special talents. They do not have to be paid back. Grants can come from federal agencies, state agencies, specific universities, and private organizations. Most federal and state grants are based on financial need.

Examples of grants are the Pell Grant, SMART Grant, and the Federal Supplemental Educational Opportunity Grant (FSEOG). Visit the US Department of Education's Federal Student Aid site for lots of current information about grants (see https://studentaid.ed.gov/types/grants-scholarships).

## SCHOLARSHIPS

Scholarships are merit-based aid that does not have to be paid back. They are typically awarded based on academic excellence or some other special talent, such as music or art. Scholarships also fall under the areas of athletic-based, minority-based, aid for women, and so forth. These are typically not awarded by federal or state governments but instead come from the specific university you applied to as well as from private and nonprofit organizations.

Be sure to reach out directly to the financial aid officers of the schools you want to attend. These people are great contacts that can lead you to many more sources of scholarships and financial aid. Visit http://www.gocollege.com /financial-aid/scholarships/types/ for lots more information about how scholarships in general work.

## LOANS

Many types of loans are available especially to students to pay for their postsecondary education. However, the important thing to remember here is that loans must be paid back, with interest. Be sure you understand the interest rate you will be charged. This is the extra cost of borrowing the money and is usually a percentage of the amount you borrow. Is this fixed or will it change over time? Is the loan and interest deferred until you graduate (meaning you don't have to begin paying it off until after you graduate)? Is the loan subsidized (meaning the federal government pays the interest until you graduate)? These are all points you need to be clear about before you sign on the dotted line.

There are many types of loans offered to students, including need-based loans, non-need-based loans, state loans, and private loans. For more information about student loans, start at https://bigfuture.collegeboard.org /pay-for-college/loans/types-of-college-loans.

## FEDERAL WORK-STUDY

The US federal work-study program provides part-time jobs for undergraduate and graduate students with financial need so they can earn money to pay for educational expenses. The focus of such work is on community service and work related to a student's course of study. Not all colleges and universities participate in this program, so be sure to check with the school financial aid office if this is something you are counting on. The sooner you apply, the more likely you are to get the job you desire and be able to benefit from the program, as funds are limited. See https://studentaid.ed.gov/sa/types/work-study for more information about this opportunity.

# COMBATING INJUSTICE AND INEQUALITY AROUND THE WORLD

Olloriak Sawade.
*Olloriak Sawade*

Olloriak Sawade was born and raised in Canada. At age fifteen, she started volunteering at a small NGO called the Kawartha World Issues Center in her local town of Peterborough, Ontario, where she learned about the struggles of the Zapatistas in Chiapas and the genocides in Rwanda. This inspired her to volunteer at an orphanage in Guatemala when she was seventeen and later pursue an honors bachelor's in international development (specialized in political administration) and then a master's degree in education in conflict. She has traveled and worked around the world and currently resides in Amsterdam, where she has worked for more than a decade for both Oxfam and Plan International.

## Why did you choose to work in the NGO/development sector?

From a young age I was struck by how injustice and inequality could exist. I couldn't understand how we could live in a world where children didn't have access to quality education or were dying from preventable diseases. I wanted a career that focused on ensuring that all children, all people, have their human rights met.

## What is a typical day on the job for you?

I have had different positions in this sector. Many internships, a policy adviser on education, manager of teams working on youth issues, knowledge manager, and currently I am a manager of a fundraising team bringing in funds for a variety of different projects. My day is mostly in front of the computer writing proposals and answering e-mails. Otherwise I am in meetings with colleagues to coordinate or coach and with potential funders to support projects. I also visit projects and talk with colleagues in different places around the world.

## What's the best part of your job?

Definitely having a chance to talk to people that have been part of a project that we have run. Hearing how people's lives have improved is incredible and very rewarding. In my day-to-day I enjoy interacting with people and brainstorming on how we can do things more effectively. I enjoy exploring new innovations in technology or methodologies that can make a bigger impact.

## What's the worst or most challenging part of your job?

The development sector is an industry like any other and has lots of politics and things that don't work effectively. This can be very frustrating, especially when you can get bogged down in bureaucracy and not be able to move as fast as you would like.

## What's the most surprising thing about your job?

That it can be like any other office job.

## What kinds of qualities do you think one needs to be successful at this job?

It helps to be a people person in my job—to be able to work well in a team and be creative and solution oriented. It also helps if you are open-minded in understanding how other cultures work.

## How do you combat burnout?

This is a real challenge in my sector because almost everyone is passionate about the work they are doing. I try to combat burnout by staying active with running and yoga. I also try to not take on more than I can handle. (Easier said than done.)

**What would you tell a young person who is thinking about getting into this sector?**

You will most likely need to do a lot of internships before you get a paid position. [It's] great if you can volunteer and work with underprivileged communities close to your home or abroad (best if you can do both). Community fundraise for projects close to your heart. Get to know other cultures and communities. It helps to have a relevant master's degree within this sector.

===

# *Summary*

This chapter covered all the aspects of college and postsecondary schooling/ certification that you'll want to consider as you move forward. Remember that finding the right fit is especially important as it increases the chances that you'll stay in school and earn your degree or certificate—and have an amazing experience while you're at it. The careers covered in this book have varying educational requirements, which means that finding the right school or program can be very different depending on your career aspirations.

In this chapter, we discussed how to evaluate and compare your options in order to get the best education for the best deal. You also learned a little about scholarships and financial aid, how the SAT and ACT tests work, if applicable, and how to write a unique personal statement that eloquently expresses your passions.

Use this chapter as a jumping-off point to dig deeper into your particular area of interest, but don't forget these important points:

- Take the SAT and ACT tests early in your junior year so you have time to take them again. Most universities automatically accept the highest scores.
- Make sure that the institution you plan to attend has an accredited program in your field of study. Some professions follow national accreditation policies, while others are state-mandated and therefore differ across state lines. Do your research and understand the differences.

- Don't underestimate how important campus visits are, especially in the pursuit of finding the right academic fit. Come prepared to ask questions not addressed on the school website or in the literature.
- Your personal statement is a very important piece of your application that can set you apart from others. Take the time and energy needed to make it unique and compelling.
- Don't assume you can't afford a school based on the sticker price. Many schools offer great scholarships and aid to qualified students. It doesn't hurt to apply. This advice especially applies to minorities, veterans, and students with disabilities.
- Don't lose sight of the fact that it's important to pursue a career that you enjoy, are good at, and are passionate about! You'll be a happier person if you do so.

At this point, your career goals and aspirations should be jelling. At the very least, you should have a plan for finding out more information. Remember to do the research about the university, school, or degree/certificate program before you reach out and especially before you visit. Faculty and staff find students who ask challenging questions much more impressive than those who ask questions that can be answered by spending ten minutes on the school website.

In chapter 4, we go into detail about the next steps—writing a résumé and cover letter, interviewing well, follow-up communications, and more. This information is not just for college grads; you can use it to secure internships, volunteer positions, summer jobs, and more. In fact, the sooner you can hone these communication skills, the better off you'll be in the professional world.

·

# 4

# *Writing Your Résumé and Interviewing*

You are now well on your way to mapping your path to achieve your career goals in the NGO sector. With each chapter of this book, we have narrowed the process from the broadest of strokes—what is the NGO sector and what kinds of jobs exist in it—to how to plan your strategy and educational approach to making your dream job a reality.

In this chapter we will cover the steps involved in applying for jobs or schools: how to prepare an effective résumé and slam-dunk an interview. Your résumé is your opportunity to summarize your experience, training, education, and goals and attract employers or school administrators. The goal of the résumé is to land the interview, and the goal of the interview is to land the job. Even if you do not have much working experience, you can still put together a résumé that expresses your interests and goals and the activities that illustrate your competence and interest.

As well as a résumé, you will be expected to write a cover letter that is basically your opportunity to reveal a little bit more about your passion and your motivation for a particular job or educational opportunity, and often to express more about you personally to give a potential employer a sense of who you are and what drives you. And particularly because you are striving for a career in a very competitive and passion-based field, it's wise to ensure your uniqueness, motivation, and commitment for working toward a meaningful cause—whatever your goal—comes through.

Giving the right impression is undoubtedly important, but don't let that make you nervous. In a résumé, cover letter, or interview, you want to put forward your best but genuine self. Dress professionally and proofread carefully, but ensure you are being yourself. In this chapter, we will cover all of these important aspects of the job-hunting process, and by the end you will feel confident and ready to present yourself as a candidate for the job you really want.

Because of the nature of work in the NGO sector, it is important to get across "soft skills," such as communication skills—both written and spoken—and interpersonal skills, which are key for working on long-term projects dealing with complex challenges like organizing resources and reporting to donors.

## *Writing Your Résumé*

Writing your first résumé can feel very challenging because you have likely not yet gained a lot of experience in a professional setting. But don't fret: employers understand that you are new to the workforce or to the particular career you are seeking. The right approach is never to exaggerate or invent experience or accomplishments but to present yourself as someone with a good work ethic and a genuine interest in the particular job or organization, and use what you can to present yourself authentically and honestly.

There are some standard elements to an effective résumé that you should be sure to include. At the top should be your name, of course, as well as your e-mail address or other contact information. Always list your experience in chronological order, beginning with your current or most recent position—or whatever experience you want to share. If you are a recent graduate with little work experience, begin with your education. If you've been in the working world for a while, you can opt to list your education or any certification you have at the end. Be sure you include any volunteer or other community service work you have done, especially if it relates to they type of work or NGO to which you are applying. The important thing is to present the most important and relevant information at the top. With only six seconds to make an impression, your résumé needs to be easy to navigate and read.

### EXPERT TIPS ON HOW TO GET AN NGO JOB

Mike Wright is director of membership and communications at Bond, the UK network for organizations working in international development. Wright provides advice for applicants, both experienced and otherwise, on how to have the best shot at getting a job with an NGO.[1] His tips:

- *Make sure your résumé is accurate.* Bond emphasizes, as mentioned earlier in this chapter, that recruiters are looking for ways to reduce the piles of résumés on their desk. Therefore, any reason to discard one is reason enough. Be sure your résumé does not contain any spelling mistakes or other errors.
- *Don't think you're God's gift to development.* Wright stresses that you should be aware that you are applying to a very competitive sector and should not expect your education or other qualifications to make you a shoo-in. There will be many applicants with the same experience and knowledge, and you should strive to make yourself stand out from that huge pack.
- *Don't rely on a résumé you wrote in 1998.* Okay, this one is not as relevant to the audience of this book, but is intended for professionals who have already been in the field for many years. Still, the advice stands: Be sure your awareness of practices in the field is as up-to-date as possible.
- *Don't be a cyber candidate only.* If you can get face-to-face with a hiring manager or someone who works in the department to which you are applying, that goes miles farther than an online application or conversation.
- *Avoid pointless jargon.* Wright writes: "Stuff like 'I'm a high-achieving, task-focused, self-starter' is meaningless. . . . I'm left just thinking 'who is this?' Applicants need to relax, describe how their experience matches the role and be more confident in being themselves."
- *Don't pigeonhole yourself into one role.* Even if you ultimately want an IT or marketing role, keep yourself open to other roles that will help you get your foot in the door. According to Wright, about one-third of the jobs are fundraising roles. Keep in mind once you are part of an organization, it is possible to transition to another role.
- *Don't be the person with the fifteen-page résumé.* Again, this is unlikely as you pursue your first job, but do keep your résumé as to-the-point as possible. Recruiters want to get a sense of you and your experience in as condensed a way as possible rather than slog through pages of padding.
- *Be prepared in the interview to talk about the organization.* Perhaps this seems obvious, but Wright says people are often unprepared to answer what should be an easy interview question: "Why do you want to work

here?" Do your research. Have a solid reason why the specific organization
to which you are applying is where you want to work. Know what they do,
how they work—anything that shows you've put time into getting to know
their mission and methods.
- *Put yourself in the recruiter's shoes.* Be a perfectionist. Write clearly and
briefly. Read your application aloud. Take your time with it and be critical. Be
sure you follow all the directions of the application process. Don't let yourself
be eliminated for careless mistakes.

Before you even begin to write your résumé, do your research. Make sure
you get a good sense of what kind of candidate or applicant a school or an
employer is looking for. You want to not only come across as competent and
qualified, you want to seem like just the right fit for just that job within that
organization.

You may need to customize your résumé for different purposes to ensure you are
not filling it with information that does not directly link to your qualifications for a
particular job.

Once you know more about the intended audience—organization, institution, or individual—of your résumé, you can begin to make a list of all the
relevant experience and education you have.

Highlight your education where you can—any courses you've taken, be it
in high school or through a community college or any other place that offers
training related to your job target. Also highlight any hobbies or volunteer experience you have—again, only as it relates to the job you are after.

> "From a young age I was struck by how injustice and inequality could exist. I couldn't understand how we could live in a world where children didn't have access to quality education or were dying from preventable diseases. I wanted a career that focused on ensuring that all children, all people, have their human rights met."—Olloriak Sawade, Oxfam

Your résumé is a document that sums up who you are and indicates in what ways you will be an asset to your future employer. But the trick is it should also be concise: one page is usually appropriate, especially for your very first résumé.

Before preparing your résumé, try to connect with a hiring professional—a human resources person or hiring manager—in a similar position or organization you are interested in. He or she can give you advice on what employers look for and what information to highlight on your résumé, as well as what types of interview questions you can expect.

As important as your résumé's content is the way you design and format it. You can find several samples online of résumés that you can be inspired by. At The Balance Careers, for example, you can find many templates and design ideas.[2] You want your résumé to be attractive to the eye and formatted in a way that makes the key points easy to spot and digest—according to some research, employers take an average of six seconds to review a résumé, so you don't have a lot of time to get across your experience and value.

## LINKING IN WITH IMPACT

As well as your paper or electronic résumé, creating a LinkedIn profile is a good way to highlight your experience and promote yourself, as well as to network. Joining professional organizations and connecting with other people in your desired field are good ways to keep abreast of changes and trends and work opportunities.

The key elements of a LinkedIn profile are your photo, your headline, and your profile summary. These are the most revealing parts of the profile and the ones employers and connections will base their impression of you on.

The photo should be carefully chosen. Remember that LinkedIn is not Facebook or Instagram: It is not the place to share a photo of you acting too casually on vacation or at a party. According to Joshua Waldman, author of *Job Searching with Social Media for Dummies*, the choice of photo should be taken seriously and be done right. His tips:

- Choose a photo in which you have a nice smile.
- Dress in professional clothing.
- Ensure the background of the photo is pleasing to the eye. According to Waldman, some colors—like green and blue—convey a feeling of trust and stability.
- Remember it's not a mug shot. You can be creative with the angle of your photo rather than stare directly into the camera.
- Use your photo to convey some aspect of your personality.
- Focus on your face. Remember, visitors to your profile will see only a small thumbnail image, so be sure your face takes up most of it.[3]

The objective of your résumé is the section at the top of your résumé that states, in a nutshell, what it you are looking for and what skills you bring to it. You many need to customize this for different applications. LiveCareer provides advice for writing objectives for various fields. In the humanitarian aid worker section, the advice is: "Skills needed for this type of position include communication, computer knowledge, analysis, commitment and teamwork. When you place an objective at the top of your résumé, you can include one of these skills in order to showcase your strengths. This will help show the interviewer right away that you're qualified for the position, as well as that you've tailored your résumé for that particular job."[4]

Your headline will appear just below your name and should summarize—in 120 characters—who you are, what you do, what you are interested in doing, and what you are motivated by. Take your time with this—it is your opportunity to sell yourself in a brief and impactful manner. Related but separate is your summary section. Here, you can share a little more about yourself than in your headline, but it should still be brief. Walman recommends your summary take no more than thirty seconds to read aloud (so yes, time yourself!); that it be short (between five and ten lines or three to five sentences), concise, and unique; and that it tell a story.

## INSPIRING STORIES

While walking on the beach one day in his native Netherlands, Merijn Everaarts was shocked to see the amount of plastic washing up from the sea. This "plastic soup," as it's called, made him wonder why anyone would buy bottled water when there is perfectly healthy water coming from the faucet. Everaarts, then an event manager, was inspired to launch a design competition in January 2010 to see who could create the ideal sustainable water bottle. The winner, Rinke van Remortel, created a bottle that was both a bottle and a cup, and when turned upside down put water on a pedestal. The bottle, now known as the Dopper, unexpectedly became Everaarts's new mission in life. But understanding that not all people have access to fresh tap water, the Dopper Foundation was created to donate Dopper water bottle projects to Simavi drinking water projects in Nepal. It's an inspiring story that illustrates that one person disturbed by one problem can take action and give others with the same concerns a platform to do the same.

## *Writing Your Cover Letter*

Along with your résumé, most employers will ask that you submit a cover letter. This is a one-page letter in which you express your motivation, why you are interested in the organization or position, and what skills you possess that make you the right fit.

Here are some tips for writing an effective cover letter:

- As always, proofread your text carefully before submitting it.
- Be sure you have a letter that is focused on a specific job. Do not make it too general or one-size-fits-all.
- Summarize why you are right for the position.
- Keep your letter to one page.
- Introduce yourself in a way that makes the reader want to know more about you and encourage them to review your résumé.
- Be specific about the job you are applying for. Mention the title and be sure it is correct.
- Try to find the name of the person who will receive your letter rather than keeping it nonspecific ("To whom it may concern").
- Be sure you include your contact details.
- End with a "call to action"—a request for an interview, for example.

## *Interviewing Skills*

With your sparkling résumé and LinkedIn profile, you are bound to be called for an interview. This is an important stage to reach: You will have already gone through several filters—a potential employer has gotten a quick scan of your experience (remember, on average a résumé is viewed for only six seconds!), has reviewed your LinkedIn profile, and has made the decision to learn more about you in person.

There's no way to know ahead of time exactly what to expect in an interview, but there are many ways to prepare yourself. You can start by learning more about the person who will be interviewing you. In the same way recruiters and employers can learn about you online, you can do the same. You can see if you have any education or work experience in common, or any contacts you both know.

A job interview can be stressful, but with the right preparation you will interview with confidence.
*Getty Images/Weekend Images Inc.*

Preparing yourself for the types of questions you will be asked to ensure you offer a thoughtful and meaningful response is vital to interview success. Consider your answers carefully and be prepared to support them with examples and anecdotes:

- Why did you decide to enter this field? What drives your passion for working within the NGO sector?
- What is your educational background? What credentials did you earn?
- What did you like best about the education experience? What did you like least?
- Where and how were you trained? What has been your best experience working with an NGO? What has been the most challenging?
- What is your management style? What management style do you prefer for your supervisor to have?

- How many employees report to you? What levels are the employees who are your direct reports?
- Are you a team player? Describe your usual role in a team-centered work environment. Do you easily assume a leadership role?

## BEWARE WHAT YOU SHARE ON SOCIAL MEDIA

Most of us engage in social media. Sites such as Facebook, Twitter, and Instagram provide us a platform for sharing photos and memories, opinions, and life events, and reveal everything from our political stance to our sense of humor. It's a great way to connect with people around the world, but once you post something, it's accessible to anyone—including potential employers—unless you take mindful precaution.

Your posts may be public, which means you may be making the wrong impression without realizing it. More and more, people are using search engines like Google to get a sense of potential employers, colleagues, or employees, and the impression you make online can have a strong impact on how you are perceived. According to the website Career Builder, 60 percent of employers search for information on candidates on social media sites.[5]

The website Glassdoor offers the following tips for how to keep your social media activity from sabotaging your career success:

- Check your privacy settings. Ensure that your photos and posts are accessible only to the friends or contacts you want to see them. You want to come across as professional and reliable.
- Rather than avoid social media while searching for a job, use it to your advantage. Give future employers a sense of your professional interests by liking pages or joining groups of professional organizations related to your career goals.
- Grammar counts. Be attentive to the quality of writing of all your posts and comments.
- Be consistent. With each social media outlet, there is a different focus and tone of what you are communicating. LinkedIn is very professional, while Facebook is far more social and relaxed. It's okay to take a different tone on various social media sites, but be sure you aren't blatantly contradicting yourself.
- Choose your username carefully. Remember, social media may be the first impression anyone has of you in the professional realm.[6]

# Dressing Appropriately

How you dress for a job interview is very important to the impression you want to make. Remember that no matter what the actual environment in which you'd be working, the interview is your chance to present your most professional self. Although you will not likely ever wear a suit to work, for the interview it's the most professional choice.

Although you may be applying for a job in a casual environment or working in the field, until the job is yours it's important to come across as a professional, including dressing the part when you interview. A suit is no longer an absolute requirement, but avoid looking too casual, as that will give the impression you are not that interested.

# What Employers Expect

Hiring managers and human resource professionals will also have certain expectations of you at an interview. The main thing is preparation: it cannot be overstated that you should arrive to an interview appropriately dressed, on time, unhurried, and ready to answer—and ask—questions.

For any job interview, the main things employers will look for are that you:

- Have a thorough understanding of the organization and the job for which you are applying.
- Be prepared to answer questions about yourself and your relevant experience.
- Be poised and likeable, but still professional. The interviewers will be looking for a sense of what it would be like to work with you on a daily basis and how your presence would fit in the culture of the business.
- Stay engaged. Listen carefully to what is being asked and offer thoughtful but concise answers. Don't blurt out answers you've memorized, but really focus on what is being asked.

- Be prepared to ask your own questions. It shows how much you understand the flow of an organization or work place and how you will contribute to it. Some questions you can ask:
  - What created the need to fill this position? Is it a new position or has someone left the organization?
  - Where does this position fit in the overall hierarchy of the organization?
  - What are the key skills required to succeed in this job?
  - What challenges might I expect to face within the first six months on the job?
  - How does this position relate to the achievement of the company's (or department's, or boss's) goals?
  - How would you describe the organization's culture?

## MOTIVATED BY MAKING A POSITIVE IMPACT

Charlene Overend.
*Charlene Overend*

Charlene Overend has worked in the voluntary sector for more than eighteen years, driven to implement positive change for organizations by creating partnerships and has a passion for working with people to create a socially responsible world. She has undertaken a number of roles, including project management, strategic planning, fundraising, and business development.

She has a particular interest in supporting schools and charities to help improve the experiences of young people while in education and to support people with disabilities.

### Why did you choose a career working in the nonprofit sector?

I guess the main reason for me to pursue a career in the sector was about making a difference to people's lives or the environment. It is knowing what I do has a positive impact and that really motivates me. However, I also knew that the voluntary sector really values all-rounders, people that can adapt, transfer their skills, and undertake a range of tasks and just get stuck in to get the job done. This really excited me as it meant there would be great opportunities for me to develop a wide range of skill sets that would benefit my career in the long term.

## What is a typical day on the job for you?

I would say I don't have a "typical" day, as my role in fundraising and business development means my day-to-day activities can vary. Some days I can be office based, working on writing funding proposals, coordinating projects, and answering telephone enquiries, while on other days I would be out having external meetings with potential funders, giving presentations about the organization, or I could be supporting colleagues to work directly with beneficiaries. This is why I love what I do—no two days could be the same.

## What's the best part of your job?

The best part of my job is building relationships with donors and funders. It is these relationships that provide the funding and pro bono support that keeps the charity operating—it is integral to the success of the organization. The feeling you get when you successfully turn these relationships into funds for the charity is unreal— especially the knowledge that everyone benefits, employees and beneficiaries.

## What's the worst or most challenging part of your job?

The most challenging element of my role goes hand in hand with the most rewarding —fundraising. In these challenging times it is getting harder and harder to find sources of funding, and the competition for these pots of money get tougher every year. When you are not successful in bringing funding it can be really upsetting, especially when you know that projects will now have to stop or beneficiary numbers reduced. However, on the positive side this does compel us as fundraisers to become more creative with our approach and find solutions—as I say, there is always a way!

## What's the most surprising thing about your job?

I am always blown away by the power and passion we get from charity supporters. Whether they benefit directly from our work or whether it is a cause close to their hearts. It would be rare to find this same passion driving other industries; it certainly is the fuel that helps drive people like me to do my best.

## What kinds of qualities do you think one needs to be successful at this job?

To be a successful fundraiser I think you need to have integrity; be a good listener; have the ability to motivate staff, volunteers, and donors; be a hard worker; have a true concern for people; have high expectations for yourself, your organization, and other people, including staff, volunteers, and donors; perseverance; and presence.

## How do you combat burnout?

Teamwork—it is as simple as that. We all look after each other in the team and share the workload evenly. I also try to build good friendships at work and incorporate some socializing and have some fun together—laughter really is the best medicine!

## What would you tell a young person who is thinking about a career in the not-for-profit sector?

Working in the charity sector is incredibly rewarding and you can build a really successful career for yourself in the process. People from all backgrounds and skill sets are needed to run this sector, meaning there is a role for everyone. I would suggest volunteering first to get some experience and to start building contacts in your network. And if you are lucky, reach out to a leader to mentor and coach you. Their insights and guidance will be invaluable. Having now worked in the sector for eighteen years, I can honestly say I have the best time—the people and the organizations have been amazing. It is great to do a job that you can be truly proud of and love.

# *Summary*

Congratulations on working through the book! You should now have a strong idea of your career goals within the NGO sector and how to realize them. In this chapter, we covered how to present yourself as the right candidate to a potential employer—and these strategies are also relevant if you are applying to a college or another form of training.

Here are some tips to sum it up:

- Your résumé should be concise and focused on only relevant aspects of your work experience or education. Although you can include some personal hobbies or details, they should be related to the job and your qualifications for it.
- Take your time with all your professional documents—your résumé, your cover letter, your LinkedIn profile—and be sure to proofread very carefully to avoid embarrassing and sloppy mistakes.

- Prepare yourself for an interview by anticipating the types of questions you will be asked and coming up with professional and meaningful responses.
- Equally, prepare some questions for your potential employer to ask at the interview. This will show you have a good understanding and interest in the organization and what role you would have in it.
- Always follow up after an interview with a letter or an e-mail. An e-mail is the fastest way to express your gratitude for the interviewer's time and restate your interest in the position.
- Dress appropriately for an interview and pay extra attention to tidiness and hygiene.
- Be wary of what you share on social media sites while job searching. Most employers research candidates online, and what you have shared will influence their idea of who you are and what it would be like to work with you.

The NGO sector is an exciting and growing one with many different types of jobs and work environments. This book has described the various jobs and provided examples of real working professionals and their impressions of what they do and how they prepared—through education or training—to do it. I hope this will further inspire you to identify your goal and know how to achieve it.

You've chosen a field that is expected to grow in the coming years and one that will offer a fulfilling, diverse, and challenging career path that will surely broaden your world view and ensure that you continue learning throughout your career. There will always be issues to tackle and others to assist in the world, and you are prepared to be part of committing yourself for working on the side of good. I wish you great success in your future.

# Notes

## Introduction

1. PayScale, "Salary for Industry: Non-Profit Organization," accessed February 10, 2020, https://www.payscale.com/research/US/Industry=Non-Profit_Organization/Salary.

2. Alexandra Mitchell, "4 Reasons to Consider a Career in NonProfits," *Fast Company*, May 28, 2015, https://www.fastcompany.com/3046552/4-reasons-to-consider-a-career-in-nonprofits.

3. Lester Salamon and Chelsea L. Newhouse, "The 2019 Nonprofit Employment Report," *Nonprofit Economic Bulletin* 47 (January 2019), http://ccss.jhu.edu/wp-content/uploads/downloads/2019/01/2019-NP-Employment-Report_FINAL_1.8.2019.pdf.

4. Brice S. McKeever, "The Nonprofit Sector in Brief 2018: Public Charities, Giving, and Volunteering," Urban Institute, November 2018, https://nccs.urban.org/publication/nonprofit-sector-brief-2018#the-nonprofit-sector-in-brief-2018-public-charites-giving-and-volunteering.

5. Ash Kumra. "Inspirational Profile: Adam Braun." Dreamitalive.com. Accessed July 15, 2020. https://www.dreamitalive.com/articles/Bestselling-Author-Pencils-of-Promise-Adam-Braun-Profile-Interview

## Chapter 1

1. Nonprofit Action, "Facts and Stats about NGOs Worldwide," September 4, 2015, http://nonprofitaction.org/2015/09/facts-and-stats-about-ngos-worldwide/.

2. NGO.org, accessed February 11, 2020, http://www.ngo.org/ngoinfo/define.html

3. Global Development Research Center, "Types of NGOs: By Orientation and Level of Operation," http://www.gdrc.org/ngo/ngo-types.html.

4. Top Nonprofits, "Top 100 Nonprofits on the Web," https://topnonprofits.com/lists/best-nonprofits-on-the-web/.

5. Nonprofit Expert, "NGOs—Non Governmental Organizations," June 16, 2017, https://www.nonprofitexpert.com/ngos-non-govermental-organizations/.

6. Furniture Bank, "Discover How Sister Anne Started Furniture Bank," June 15, 2014, https://www.furniturebank.org/discover-sister-anne-started-furniture-bank/.

7. Peter Hall-Jones, "The Rise and Rise of NGOs," *Global Policy Forum*, May 2006, https://www.globalpolicy.org/component/content/article/176/31937.html.

8. Jesus Bradley, "10 Largest Non-Profit Organizations of the World," Public Interest Foundation, January 13, 2019, https://publicinterestfoundation.com/10-largest-non-profit-organizations-of-the-world/.

9. Alexandra Mitchell, "4 Reasons to Consider a Career in Nonprofits," *Fast Company*, May 28, 2015, https://www.fastcompany.com/3046552/4-reasons-to-consider-a-career-in-nonprofits.

10. Cheryl Chamberlain, "Millennials Are Geared to Create Impactful Change in the Nonprofit Sector," *Forbes*, June 11, 2018, https://www.forbes.com/sites/forbesnonprofitcouncil/2018/06/11/millennials-are-geared-to-create-impactful-change-in-the-nonprofit-sector/#60c6c6171098.

11. Indeed.com, "Program Officer Salaries in the United States," https://www.indeed.com/salaries/program-officer-Salaries.

12. Indeed.com, "Program Assistant Salaries in the United States," https://www.indeed.com/salaries/program-assistant-Salaries.

13. Indeed.com, "Financial Specialist Salaries in the United States," https://www.indeed.com/salaries/financial-specialist-Salaries.

14. Indeed.com, "Policy Manager Salaries in the United States," https://www.indeed.com/salaries/policy-manager-Salaries.

15. Indeed.com, "Program Director Salaries in the United States," https://www.indeed.com/salaries/program-director-Salaries.

16. Indeed.com, "Program Coordinator Salaries in the United States," https://www.indeed.com/salaries/program-coordinator-Salaries.

17. US Bureau of Labor Statistics, "Fundraisers," https://www.bls.gov/ooh/business-and-financial/fundraisers.htm.

# Chapter 2

1. Sheryl Burgstahler, Sara Lopez, and Scott Bellman, "Preparing for a Career: An Online Tutorial," DO-IT, https://www.washington.edu/doit/preparing-career-online-tutorial.

2. Ryan Libre, "How to Start a Successful NGO in Ten Steps," *Matador Network*, September 7, 2008, https://matadornetwork.com/change/how-to-start-a-successful-ngo-in-10-steps/.

3. Suzanne Bearne, "How to Find a Career in Humanitarian and International Relief Work," *Guardian*, September 21, 2016, https://www.theguardian.com/careers /2016/sep/21/how-to-find-a-career-in-humanitarian-and-international-relief-work.

# Chapter 3

1. National Center for Education Statistics, "Fast Facts: Graduation Rates," https://nces.ed.gov/fastfacts/display.asp?id=40.

2. US Department of Education, "Focusing Higher Education on Student Success," July 27, 2015, https://www.ed.gov/news/press-releases/fact-sheet-focusing -higher-education-student-success.

3. Department of Education, National Center for Education Statistics, "Table 502.30: Median Annual Earnings of Full-Time Year-Round Workers 25 to 34 Years Old and Full-Time Year-Round Workers as a Percentage of the Labor Force, by Sex, Race/ Ethnicity, and Educational Attainment: Selected Years, 1995 through 2013," *Digest for Education Statistics*, https://nces.ed.gov/programs/digest/d14/tables/dt14_502.30.asp; Bureau of Labor Statistics, Current Population Survey, "Employment Status of the Civilian Noninstitutional Population 25 Years and Over by Educational Attainment, Sex, Race, and Hispanic or Latino Identity," http://www.bls.gov/cps/cpsaat07.htm.

4. US Department of Education, *Web Tables: Transfer, Retention, and Withdrawal Rates of Students Who Began Postsecondary Education in 2003–04*, July 2011, https:// nces.ed.gov/pubs2011/2011152.pdf

5. Dr. Steven R. Antonoff, "College Personality Quiz," *U.S. News & World Report*, July 31, 2018, https://www.usnews.com/education/best-colleges/right-school /choices/articles/college-personality-quiz.

6. Anu Prasad, "12 Lessons from My Year as a Start-Up NGO Founder," *SheThePeople*, December 24, 2008, https://www.shethepeople.tv/top-stories/12-lessons -year-startup-ngo-founder-anu-prasad/.

7. fafsa.gov

# Chapter 4

1. Mike Wright, "Tips to Get an NGO Job." Bond, November 23, 2016, https:// www.bond.org.uk/news/2016/11/tips-to-get-an-ngo-job.

2. Alison Doyle, "Student Resume Examples, Templates, and Writing Tips," *The Balance Careers*, https://www.thebalancecareers.com/student-resume-examples -and-templates-2063555.

3. Joshua Waldman, *Job Searching with Social Media for Dummies* (Hoboken, NJ: Wiley and Sons, 2013), 148–149.

4. LiveCareer, "Humanitarian Aid Worker Resume Objective Sample," https:// www.livecareer.com/resumes/objectives/humanitarian-aid-worker-resume-objective.

5. Career Builder, http://www.careerbuilder.com/share/aboutus/pressreleases detail.aspx?ed=12%2F31%2F2016&id=pr945&sd=4%2F28%2F2016.

6. Alice A. M. Underwood, "9 Things to Avoid on Social Media While Looking for a New Job," January 3, 2018, https://www.glassdoor.com/blog/things-to-avoid-on -social-media-job-search/.

# Glossary

**bachelor's degree:** A four-year degree awarded by a college or university.

**bureaucratic:** Something governed by many different players or processes that forestall progress.

**burnout:** The feeling of physical and emotional exhaustion caused by overworking.

**campus:** The physical location of a school, college, or university.

**career assessment test:** A test that asks questions particularly geared to identify skills and interests to help inform test takers about what type of career would suit them.

**colleagues:** The people alongside whom you work.

**community college:** A two-year college that awards associate's degrees.

**cover letter:** A document that usually accompanies a résumé in which candidates applying for a job or to a school or internship describe their motivation and qualifications.

**educational background:** The degrees a person has earned and schools attended.

**entrepreneur:** A person who creates, launches, and manages his or her own business.

**financial aid:** Various means of financial support for the purposes of attending school, including grants and scholarships, for example.

**for-profit organizations:** Organizations that work to make a profit and must pay taxes on the money they earn.

**freelancer:** A person who owns his or her own business that provides services for a variety of clients.

**fundraising:** The act of raising money to support an NGO and its projects.

**gap year:** A year between high school and higher education or employment during which a person can explore his or her passions and interests, often while traveling.

**General Educational Development (GED):** An exam that confers a credential that is the equivalent to a high school diploma without graduating from a traditional high school.

**internship:** A work experience opportunity that lasts for a set period of time and can be paid or unpaid.

**interpersonal skills:** The ability to communicate and interact with other people in an effective manner.

**interviewing:** A part of the job-seeking process in which a candidate meets with a potential employer, usually face-to-face, in order to discuss the candidate's work experience and education and seek information about the position.

**information technology (IT):** The use of computers to store, retrieve, transmit, and manipulate data.

**job market:** The total number of vacant jobs open to those seeking employment.

**major:** The subject or course of study in which a student chooses to earn a degree.

**master's degree:** A degree that is sought by those who have already earned a bachelor's degree in order to further their education.

**networking:** The processes of building, strengthening, and maintaining professional relationships as a way to further one's career goals.

**nongovernmental organizations (NGOs):** Nonprofit organizations that usually focus on social issues and are independent of governments.

**nonprofit organizations:** Businesses that do not pay taxes on received donations or any other money earned through fundraising activities.

**on-the-job training:** A type of training in which a person is learning while actually doing the job in a real-world environment.

**profit:** The difference between money spent to create a product or service and money gained from it.

**red tape:** A term for an overload of policies and rules that prevent work from getting accomplished quickly and effectively.

**résumé:** A document, usually one page, that outlines a person's professional experience and education and is designed to give potential employers a sense of a candidate's qualifications.

**sector:** An area that is specific and set apart from other types of work or organization, such as the NGO sector.

**social causes:** Causes or issues that have an impact on a large part of a society.

**social media:** Websites and applications that enable users to create and share content online for networking and social-sharing purposes. Examples include Facebook and Instagram.

**tax-exempt:** A status describing a business that does not have to pay taxes.

**tuition:** The money a student has to pay for education, be it a university degree or a certification.

**volunteer:** A person who does work without being paid a salary.

**work culture:** A concept that describes the beliefs, philosophy, thought processes, and attitudes of employees in a particular organization.

# Resources

The following websites, magazines, and organizations can help you further investigate and educate yourself on NGO-related topics, all of which will help you as you take the next steps in your career, now and throughout.

## Professional Organizations

*World Association of Non-Governmental Organizations (WANGO)*
https://www.wango.org
An international organization that unites NGOs worldwide with the goal of advancing peace and global well-being.

*International NGO Safety and Security Association (INSSA)*
https://inssa.org
A nonprofit global membership association of individuals committed to improving the quality and effectiveness of safety and security for humanitarian relief and development assistance workers operating in complex and dangerous environments.

*International Federation of Social Workers (IFSW)*
https://www.ifsw.org/
The global body for the social work profession; it has consultative status with United Nations Economic and Social Council and partners with various NGOs.

*CoNGO*
www.ngocongo.org
CoNGO's aim is to be the primary support and platform for a civil society represented by a global community of informed, empowered, and committed

NGOs that fully participate with the UN in decision making and programs leading to a better world, a world of economic and social justice.

*International Council on Social Welfare (ICSW)*
https://icsw.org/
An international nongovernmental organization operating throughout the world for the cause of social welfare, social justice, and social development.

*Peace Corps*
https://www.peacecorps.gov/
If you are interested in taking a gap year before taking the next step in your career or education, consider joining the Peace Corps. Volunteers have the experience of working on projects that relate to health, agriculture, education, and youth and development, just to name a few, and the experience can help you find your passion and understand what the next step in your life should be.

# *Magazines*

*Global Education*
http://www.globaleducationmagazine.com/
An educational e-journal with international character that seeks to promote ideas and experiences from the work of educational professionals, as well as NGOs.

*Nonprofit Quarterly*
https://nonprofitquarterly.org
Provides in-depth, researched-based information relating to critical issues facing the nonprofit community.

*Advancing Philanthropy*
https://afpglobal.org/
A print and digital magazine published by the Association of Fundraising Professionals (AFP). Suitable for anyone involved in fundraising, the magazine comes out five times a year.

*Alliance*

https://www.alliancemagazine.org/magazine/

Provides global coverage with emphasis on subjects such as the economic issues as they relate to social entrepreneurship, international development, and philanthropy.

*Chronicle of Philanthropy*

https://www.philanthropy.com

Provides the latest news on the nonprofit world, including information about job postings.

*Global Journal*

http://www.theglobaljournal.net

A daily online magazine committed to bringing attention to the inspiring work being done by NGOs on a daily basis.

# Bibliography

AllAboutCareers. "Charity, Not-for-Profit and NGO Careers." https://www
.allaboutcareers.com/careers/industry/charity-not-for-profit-ngo.

Antonoff, Dr. Steven R. "College Personality Quiz." *U.S. News & World
Report*, July 31, 2018. https://www.usnews.com/education/best-colleges
/right-school/choices/articles/college-personality-quiz.

Bearne, Suzanne. "How to Find a Career in Humanitarian and International
Relief Work." *Guardian*, September 21, 2016. https://www.theguardian
.com/careers/2016/sep/21/how-to-find-a-career-in-humanitarian-and
-international-relief-work.

Bradley, Jesus. "10 Largest Non-Profit Organizations of the World." Public
Interest Foundation, January 13, 2019. https://publicinterestfoundation
.com/10-largest-non-profit-organizations-of-the-world/.

Bright Network. "Seven Types of Roles within the Charity Sector." https://www
.brightnetwork.co.uk/career-path-guides/charity-NGO-social-enterprise
/roles-in-charity/.

Career Builder. http://www.careerbuilder.com/share/aboutus/pressreleases
detail.aspx?ed=12%2F31%2F2016&id=pr945&sd=4%2F28%2F2016.

Chamberlain, Cheryl. "Millennials Are Geared to Create Impactful Change
in the Nonprofit Sector." *Forbes*, June 11, 2018. https://www.forbes.com
/sites/forbesnonprofitcouncil/2018/06/11/millennials-are-geared-to
-create-impactful-change-in-the-nonprofit-sector/#63392ddc1098.

Doyle, Alison. "Student Resume Examples, Templates, and Writing Tips."
*The Balance Careers*. https://www.thebalancecareers.com/student-resume
-examples-and-templates-2063555.

Furniture Bank. "Discover How Sister Anne Started Furniture Bank."
June 15, 2014. https://www.furniturebank.org/discover-sister-anne-started
-furniture-bank/.

Global Development Research Center. "Types of NGOs: By Orientation and
Level of Operation." https://www.gdrc.org/ngo/ngo-types.html.

Hall-Jones, Peter. "The Rise and Rise of NGOs." *Global Policy Forum*, May 2006. https://www.globalpolicy.org/component/content/article/176/31937 .html.

Indeed.com. "Financial Specialist Salaries in the United States." https://www .indeed.com/salaries/financial-specialist-Salaries.

———. "Policy Manager Salaries in the United States." https://www.indeed .com/salaries/policy-manager-Salaries.

———. "Program Assistant Salaries in the United States." https://www.indeed .com/salaries/program-assistant-Salaries.

———. "Program Coordinator Salaries in the United States." https://www .indeed.com/salaries/program-coordinator-Salaries.

———. "Program Director Salaries in the United States." https://www.indeed .com/salaries/program-director-Salaries.

———. "Program Officer Salaries in the United States." https://www.indeed .com/salaries/program-officer-Salaries.

Kumra, Ash. "Inspirational Profile: Adam Braun." DreamItAlive. https://www .dreamitalive.com/articles/Bestselling-Author-Pencils-of-Promise-Adam -Braun-Profile-Interview.

Libre, Ryan. "How to Start a Successful NGO in Ten Steps." *Matador Network*, September 7, 2008. https://matadornetwork.com/change/how-to-start -a-successful-ngo-in-10-steps/.

LiveCareer. "Humanitarian Aid Worker Resume Objective Sample." https:// www.livecareer.com/resumes/objectives/humanitarian-aid-worker -resume-objective.

McKeever, Brice S. "The Nonprofit Sector in Brief 2018: Public Charities, Giving, and Volunteering." Urban Institute, November 2018. https://nccs .urban.org/publication/nonprofit-sector-brief-2018#the-nonprofit-sector -in-brief-2018-public-charites-giving-and-volunteering.

Mitchell, Alexandra. "4 Reasons to Consider a Career in Nonprofits." *Fast Company*, May 28, 2015. https://www.fastcompany.com/3046552/4 -reasons-to-consider-a-career-in-nonprofits.

NGO.org. Accessed February 11, 2020. http://www.ngo.org/ngoinfo/define .html

Nonprofit Action. "Facts and Stats about NGOs Worldwide." September 4, 2015. http://nonprofitaction.org/2015/09/facts-and-stats-about-ngos-world wide/.

Nonprofit Expert. "NGOs—Non Governmental Organizations." June 16, 2017.
    https://www.nonprofitexpert.com/ngos-non-govermental-organizations/.
PayScale. "Salary for Industry: Non-Profit Organization." Accessed February
    10, 2020. https://www.payscale.com/research/US/Industry=Non-Profit
    _Organization/Salary.
Prasad, Anu. "12 Lessons from My Year as a Start-up NGO Founder."
    *SheThePeople*, December 24, 2008. https://www.shethepeople.tv/top
    -stories/12-lessons-year-startup-ngo-founder-anu-prasad/.
Salamon, Lester, and Chelsea L. Newhouse. "The 2019 Nonprofit Employment
    Report." *Nonprofit Economic Bulletin* 47 (January 2019). http://ccss
    .jhu.edu/wp-content/uploads/downloads/2019/01/2019-NP-Employ
    ment-Report_FINAL_1.8.2019.pdf.
Top Nonprofits. "Top 100 Nonprofits on the Web." https://topnonprofits
    .com/lists/best-nonprofits-on-the-web/.
Underwood, Alice A. M. "9 Things to Avoid on Social Media while Looking
    for a New Job." Glassdoor, January 3, 2018. https://www.glassdoor.com
    /blog/things-to-avoid-on-social-media-job-search/.
US Bureau of Labor Statistics. "Fundraisers." https://www.bls.gov/ooh/busi
    ness-and-financial/fundraisers.htm.
US Department of State, Bureau of Democracy, Human Rights, and Labor.
    "Non-Governmental Organizations (NGOs) in the United States."
    January 20, 2017. https://www.state.gov/non-governmental-organizations
    -ngos-in-the-united-states/.
Waldman, Joshua. *Job Searching with Social Media for Dummies*. Hoboken, NJ:
    Wiley and Sons, 2013.
Wright, Mike. "Tips to Get an NGO Job." Bond, November 23, 2016. https://
    www.bond.org.uk/news/2016/11/tips-to-get-an-ngo-job.

# About the Author

**Tracy Brown Hamilton** is a writer, editor, and journalist based in the Netherlands. She has written several books on topics ranging from careers to media, economics to pop culture. She lives with her husband and three children.